# Equipped for God's Work

*How God Prepares His People for Service*

By Matthew Allen

Published by
Spiritbuilding Publishers
9700 Ferry Road, Waynesville, OH 45068

EQUIPPED FOR GOD'S WORK
How God Prepares His People for Service
By Matthew Allen

ISBN: 978–1–964–80564–1

# Spiritbuilding

## PUBLISHERS

spiritbuilding.com

# Table of Contents

Introduction . . . . . . . . . . . . . . . . . . . . . . . . . . . . . . . . . . . . . . . . . . . . . . 1

How to Use This Workbook . . . . . . . . . . . . . . . . . . . . . . . . . . . . 3

**Part 1 God's Call to Serve** . . . . . . . . . . . . . . . . . . . . . . . . . . . . . . 7

   1   The God Who Equips the Called . . . . . . . . . . . . . . . . . . . . . 8

   2   Moses: Strength Made Perfect in Weakness . . . . . . . . . . . 18

   3   Joshua: Courage for the Task . . . . . . . . . . . . . . . . . . . . . . . 29

   4   Gideon: God's Power in Our Weakness . . . . . . . . . . . . . . . 40

   5   Samuel: Hearing God's Call . . . . . . . . . . . . . . . . . . . . . . . . 51

**Part 2 Prepared by Providence** . . . . . . . . . . . . . . . . . . . . . . . . . 63

   6   Esther: For Such a Time as This . . . . . . . . . . . . . . . . . . . . . 64

   7   David: Equipped in the Fields . . . . . . . . . . . . . . . . . . . . . . 75

   8   Nehemiah: A Heart to Build . . . . . . . . . . . . . . . . . . . . . . . 85

   9   Daniel: Standing Firm in a Shifting World . . . . . . . . . . . 96

**Part 3 Strengthened for the Mission** . . . . . . . . . . . . . . . . . . . . 107

   10   Mary: Faith to Surrender . . . . . . . . . . . . . . . . . . . . . . . . . 108

   11   Peter: Strengthened After Failure . . . . . . . . . . . . . . . . . . 118

   12   Paul: Bold for the Gospel . . . . . . . . . . . . . . . . . . . . . . . . . 127

   13   Jesus: The Perfect Example . . . . . . . . . . . . . . . . . . . . . . . . 137

Conclusion . . . . . . . . . . . . . . . . . . . . . . . . . . . . . . . . . . . . . . . . . . . 146

# Introduction

Every generation of believers must learn again that God does His greatest work through ordinary people who are willing to trust Him. Scripture is filled with men and women who were called, shaped, tested, and strengthened for a purpose larger than themselves. Their stories remind us that faith is a life of obedience.

This study, *Equipped for God's Work*, traces that truth through the lives of faithful servants across the Bible. From Noah to Jesus, we see that God never calls without also equipping. He prepares hearts before He sends hands. Each lesson shows a different aspect of how God works in His people to accomplish His will: faith that obeys, courage that endures, grace that restores, and surrender that trusts.

Our goal in this series is not simply to admire their faith, but to develop our own. The same God who strengthened Noah to build, Joshua to lead, and Mary to believe is still shaping His people today. Every challenge, every act of obedience, and every step of faith is part of His process of equipping us for service in His kingdom.

As you study these lessons, you'll see that:

- **Faith** begins with trust in God's promises.
- **Obedience** turns faith into action.
- **Grace** restores the fallen and strengthens the weary.
- **Courage** grows when we keep our eyes on the Lord.
- **Endurance** carries us to the finish.

This workbook is designed to help you see how God prepares His servants, and how He is preparing you. Each lesson includes clear biblical teaching, practical application, and reflection questions to help you take these truths from Scripture into daily life.

Let every page remind you that you are not unequipped or alone. The same Spirit who worked in these faithful men and women now works in you. God's plan for your life is not limited by your weakness but empowered by His strength.

*Now these things happened to them as examples, and they were written for our instruction, on whom the ends of the ages have come.*
**1 Corinthians 10:11 (CSB)**

Matthew Allen

November 2025

# How to Use This Workbook

This workbook is designed to help you grow in faith, character, and service as you study the lives of men and women God equipped for His work. Each lesson is structured to guide you through Scripture, reflection, and personal application. The goal is to become more like the God who shaped them.

## 1. Read the Lesson Carefully

Each lesson includes background information, teaching points, and biblical insights. Read thoughtfully. Take your time with the Scripture references and allow the message of God's Word to speak for itself before turning to the commentary.

## 2. Reflect on the Main Points

After reading, take a few moments to summarize what stands out to you. Each point is meant to highlight a key truth about faith, obedience, or endurance. Ask how these truths apply to your life, your church, and your daily walk with God.

## 3. Review the Key Verse

Every lesson includes a memory verse that captures its central message. Read it aloud. Write it down. Pray over it. Hiding God's Word in your heart will help you carry these lessons beyond the classroom.

## 4. Engage with the Weekly Challenge

The weekly challenge gives you a way to live out what you've learned. These simple actions, serving, praying, reflecting, or encouraging, turn faith into practice. Growth happens when truth moves from the page to your life.

## 5. Use the Reflection Questions

Each lesson ends with discussion or reflection questions. Use them to deepen your study personally or as a group. They are written to prompt honest thought and conversation about how these biblical principles fit real life.

### 6. Pray as You Study

Ask God to shape your heart as He shaped the lives you are studying. Prayer invites transformation. Before and after each lesson, pause to thank Him for what He is teaching you and to ask for strength to obey.

### 7. Share What You Learn

Faith grows stronger when shared. Discuss these lessons with others in your congregation, family, or study group. Encourage one another to live as servants who are equipped for God's work.

### A Final Word

God is still forming His people into instruments of His grace. As you walk through these pages, remember that you are part of the same story. The God who called Noah to build, David to lead, Mary to trust, and Paul to preach is calling you to serve today.

*For we are His workmanship, created in Christ Jesus for good works, which God prepared ahead of time for us to do.*
**Ephesians 2:10 (CSB)**

# PART ONE

# God's Call to Serve

*When God calls His people to serve, He always provides the strength and resources needed to fulfill that call. The December lessons will trace how God chose and equipped His servants in the Old Testament, revealing that His work has never depended on human ability but on divine power and faith.*

*We begin with Moses' encounter at the burning bush, where God assured him, "I will certainly be with you" (Exodus 3:12). From Moses' reluctant obedience to Joshua's courageous leadership, we see that God supplies what His servants lack. Gideon's story reminds us that the Lord uses weakness to display His strength, while young Samuel teaches us the importance of listening to God's voice and responding in faith. Each of these stories reveals that when God calls, He also equips—turning ordinary people into vessels of extraordinary purpose.*

# The God Who Equips the Called
### Exodus 3:1–12

*Therefore, go. I am sending you to Pharaoh so that you may lead my people,
the Israelites, out of Egypt." But Moses asked God, "Who am I that I should
go to Pharaoh and that I should bring the Israelites out of Egypt?"
He answered, "I will certainly be with you, and this will be the sign to you
that I have sent you: when you bring the people out of Egypt,
you will all worship God at this mountain.*
### Exodus 3:10–12

**Class Overview:** Moses' encounter at the burning bush shows that God
never calls someone without also providing what they need to serve.
When God chose Moses to lead Israel out of Egypt, Moses protested his
inadequacy. Yet God answered each fear with His presence and promise:
"I will certainly be with you." This lesson reminds us that God's strength
is always greater than our weakness. The same Lord who equipped
Moses to confront Pharaoh equips His people today through His Word,
His Spirit, and His faithful presence to do what He commands.

**Class Objectives:** By the end of this class, you should be able to—

1. Recognize that God's calling always includes His equipping.
2. Understand the significance of Moses' encounter with God in
   Exodus 3.
3. Identify the excuses Moses made and how God answered each one.
4. Explain how God's presence empowers believers for service today.
5. Commit to trusting God's ability more than personal ability when
   called to serve.

# Introduction

WHEN EXODUS 3 BEGINS, Moses is an elderly man with calloused hands and a quiet life. For forty years, he has lived in the wilderness, far from Egypt's influence and suffering. Any dreams he once had of saving his people are gone. He has settled into obscurity, tending sheep that don't even belong to him. Yet it is here, in weakness, not strength, that God chooses to speak.

The burning bush scene is not about Moses' greatness but God, who interrupts an ordinary day to reveal His extraordinary purpose. The bush burns without being consumed, a sign of divine presence that cannot be diminished. Moses draws near, curious, and suddenly hears his name: "Moses, Moses." That moment changes everything.

Divine assignments often start where human confidence ends. Moses feels unqualified: "Who am I that I should go to Pharaoh?" (Exodus 3:11). But God's response is everything: "I will certainly be with you." God's presence, not human ability, is what equips His servants. The lesson is timeless. When God calls us to serve, He doesn't require perfection; He asks for trust. He provides the strength, wisdom, and courage we lack. God delights in using ordinary people who rely completely on Him. Every Christian is called to some form of service, and every calling comes with His promise: "I am with you always."

## *Historical Background*

The events of Exodus 3 occur around the early 13th century B.C., long after Joseph's generation had died and Israel had multiplied into a large nation enslaved by Egypt. Pharaoh viewed the Hebrews as a threat to his empire and subjected them to cruel labor. The cries of God's people rose up to heaven, and the text says, "God heard their groaning ... and remembered His covenant with Abraham, Isaac, and Jacob" (Exodus 2:24).

Moses was born into a time of oppression. Rescued from Pharaoh's order to kill Hebrew infants, he was raised in the royal palace but never lost sight of his identity. At forty, he killed an Egyptian who was beating a Hebrew slave and fled to save his life. He then spent the next forty years in Midian, marrying Zipporah, Jethro's daughter, and working as a shepherd. In Egypt, he was powerful; in Midian, he became humble. God was shaping him through obscurity and hardship so he would depend on Him alone.

Mount Horeb, also called Mount Sinai, was a rugged, desolate area. The "angel of the Lord" appearing in the burning bush is identified as God Himself speaking from the flame. This theophany revealed God's holiness ("Remove your sandals, for the place where you are standing is holy ground"), His compassion ("I have seen the suffering of My people"), and His purpose ("I am sending you to Pharaoh"). The name "I AM WHO I AM" (Yahweh) revealed the eternal, self-existent nature of God—the One who was, is, and always will be.

The meeting at Horeb transformed a wandering shepherd into God's chosen leader. What seemed like failure and exile had been preparation. Through His presence, promises, and power, God was equipping Moses to accomplish what human strength alone never could.

## God Calls Ordinary People in Ordinary Moments

Exodus 3 begins with Moses doing the same thing he had done every day for forty years: tending sheep in the wilderness. It was routine work, far from the Egyptian royal court. But that's exactly where God met him. The scene couldn't have been more ordinary: a shepherd, a desert, a flock. Yet the moment was extraordinary because God chose to speak. The burning bush burned without being consumed. When Moses turned aside to look, God called his name twice, "Moses, Moses." The call was personal and direct. God didn't wait for Moses to be in a temple or prayer meeting; He met him at work.

Moses' situation teaches us a lot about how God works. By this time in his life, Moses was around eighty years old and living as a foreigner. His dreams of leading Israel had faded many years earlier. He didn't even own the sheep he was watching; they belonged to his father-in-law. Still, none of that mattered to God. The Lord doesn't seek prestige, youth, or strength. He looks for hearts that are willing to listen. God often calls people when they feel their best years are behind them. He finds them in ordinary situations and redirects their focus toward His purpose.

This pattern repeats throughout Scripture. Gideon was threshing wheat when God called him a "valiant warrior." Samuel was asleep when he first heard God's voice. David was tending his father's sheep when Samuel anointed him king. Amos was caring for sycamore trees when the Lord sent him to prophesy. The disciples were fishing or collecting taxes when Jesus said, "Follow Me." Mary was living quietly in Nazareth when she learned she would bear the Son of God. Time and again, God calls people in the middle of ordinary life.

The theology here is simple but powerful. *God's calling is based on His choice, not our qualifications.* God often calls after periods of failure or waiting because those are times when pride has diminished and faith can grow. The first step of obedience is paying attention. We have to turn to see what God is doing and say, "Here I am."

Many of us resist God's call for the same reasons Moses did. We think we're too old, too busy, or too unqualified. We assume our routine is too mundane for God to use. But the story of Moses reminds us that God shapes servants in quiet places long before He sends them to great ones. He trains hearts through everyday faithfulness. That means every job, every errand, every unnoticed act of service can be a training ground for divine work.

We need to live with open eyes and hearts. Treat your daily path as potential sacred ground. Invite God into the routines of your week: the commute, the conversations, the chores. Small acts of attention can open doors for extraordinary acts of faith. God is still calling ordinary people in ordinary moments. The question is whether we will stop, turn aside, and say, "Here I am."

## God Reveals His Presence
## Before He Gives the Mission

Before Moses ever received a command, he received a revelation. God's first words to him were not about Pharaoh or Israel; they were about holiness. As Moses approached the burning bush, a voice called out, "Do not come closer. Remove the sandals from your feet, for the place where you are standing is holy ground" (Exodus 3:5). Note how God revealed who He is before explaining what He wanted Moses to do. *Service always begins with reverence.* Before we can represent God, we must recognize His holiness and authority.

While the burning bush served as a visual wonder, it was a lesson about God's nature. The bush burned but was not consumed, symbolizing God's power that never fades and His purity that cannot be diminished. The same fire that later descended on Sinai and filled the tabernacle was first seen here in miniature. It reminded Moses that the God of Abraham, Isaac, and Jacob was alive, eternal, and unchanging. The fire that drew Moses' attention would become the same presence that guided Israel through the wilderness by pillar of fire and cloud.

Moses needed this encounter before he could ever stand before Pharaoh. The task ahead was enormous, but God grounded Moses' courage in His character. When Moses asked, "Who am I that I should go to Pharaoh and bring the Israelites out of Egypt?" (Exodus 3:11), God did not boost Moses' confidence or list his qualifications. Instead, He gave the only answer that mattered: "I will certainly be with you" (v. 12). The power to serve did not come from Moses' abilities but from God's abiding presence.

This truth runs throughout all of Scripture. When Joshua took over from Moses, God said, "I will be with you, just as I was with Moses" (Joshua 1:5). When Gideon was afraid of his task, the Lord said, "I will be with you" (Judges 6:16). When Jesus sent out His disciples to make disciples of all nations, He promised, "I am with you always, to the end of the age" (Matthew 28:20). God's servants find their courage not from what they can do, but from who is with them.

Our culture often encourages us to look inward for strength, but Scripture directs us to look upward. God's presence is the foundation of faith and the power behind every mission. When we begin with worship, we remember that service flows from relationship. We are not doing God's work for Him; *we are doing His work with Him,* and reverence grounds obedience. If we forget God's holiness, our service can become mechanical or self-centered. But when we remember who He is, even the hardest tasks can become opportunities for His glory to shine.

We need to slow down before serving. God cares more about shaping our hearts than filling our schedules. He wants His people to realize that true effectiveness comes from communion with Him, not from human effort. Before we speak for God, we must stand before Him. Before we go, we must worship. And when we do, we learn what Moses discovered that day at the bush: God's presence is enough.

## God's Power Overcomes Human Weakness

When Moses heard God's call, his first instinct was to resist. "Who am I that I should go to Pharaoh?" he asked (Exodus 3:11). Those words reveal a man deeply aware of his inadequacy. Moses understood the weight of failure. He had fled Egypt decades earlier, a fugitive and a disappointment to his people. His confidence was gone. In human terms, he was the least likely candidate to confront Pharaoh, the world's most powerful man. But God wasn't looking for a hero: He was looking for a vessel.

God's response to Moses' fear was simple: "I will certainly be with you." That promise shifts the focus from the servant's weakness to the Sender's strength. God never denied Moses' shortcomings. Instead, He filled the gaps with His own power. Moses' sense of inadequacy became the very reason God could use him. A proud, self-reliant man might have tried to lead by force; a humbled man would learn to depend completely on God. Weakness, in God's hands, becomes a tool for His glory.

Later in their conversation, Moses raised more objections: he feared the people's doubts, his lack of eloquence, and his inability to persuade. Each time, God responded by revealing more of Himself. When Moses said, "They will ask me, 'What is His name?'" God replied, "I AM WHO I AM." Those words affirm the eternal, self-existent nature of God. He is not defined by time, place, or power. His name means "the One who is." The success of the mission would depend entirely on who God is, not on who Moses was.

In Scripture, God consistently chooses the weak to show His strength. He used a shepherd boy to defeat a giant, a reluctant prophet to confront a king, a teenage girl to bear the Messiah, and untrained fishermen to turn the world upside down. Paul said, "But he said to me, 'My grace is sufficient for you, for my power is perfected in weakness'" (2 Corinthians 12:9). God doesn't remove our frailty; He works through it.

Many Christians today hesitate to serve because they feel unqualified. We worry that we don't know enough, speak well enough, or lead confidently enough. But those excuses resemble Moses' words at the bush. God still responds the same way: "I will be with you." He equips us through His Word, His Spirit, and His people. He provides what we lack when we trust Him enough to step forward. Our weakness becomes the stage on which His strength is displayed.

We need to shift our confidence from ourselves to the Savior. God's work has never relied on human ability; it depends on His power working through surrendered hearts. Moses went from being a fearful man hiding in the desert to a bold leader confronting Pharaoh—not because he found hidden courage, but because he learned to depend on God's strength. The same God who transformed Moses is working in us. When we feel the least capable, we're often closest to being useful. God's grace fills every gap created by our weakness.

## Lesson Summary and Reflection

Moses' call at the burning bush reminds us that God always prepares before sending. God meets people in everyday moments, reveals His presence before giving a task, and provides His strength to overcome weakness. What started as an ordinary day for Moses became a defining moment because he paused to listen. The same God who spoke from the bush still calls His people today, often when life feels routine or when we feel most unqualified.

When God revealed Himself to Moses, He emphasized holiness, compassion, and presence. He reminded Moses that His plan was not dependent on human strength or skill. The call to serve always begins with knowing who God is. Before Moses could stand before Pharaoh, he had to bow before the Lord. That order never changes. True service grows out of worship. God wants servants who depend on Him, not themselves.

Each objection Moses raised: his fear, his lack of eloquence, his sense of failure, was answered by one truth: "I will certainly be with you." Those words remain the heart of every calling. God's presence is our greatest support. It helps us overcome fear, doubt, and hard times. When we realize this, we stop judging our ability and start trusting Him.

Divine work does not require extraordinary talent but a willing heart. God uses ordinary people, shepherds, laborers, parents, teachers, and retirees to accomplish His purpose. He equips them through His Word, His Spirit, and His providence. Like Moses, we must learn to listen, trust, and obey even when the journey seems challenging. God takes pleasure in demonstrating His power through humble servants who are ready to say, "Here I am."

### Key Truths

- God calls ordinary people amid ordinary life.
- Every calling begins with recognizing God's presence and holiness.
- God's strength always exceeds human weakness.
- The promise of "I will be with you" is the foundation for faithful service.
- True service grows out of reverence, dependence, and trust in God's sufficiency.

# Conclusion

Divine work is never about our ability; it is about His presence. He doesn't choose the strongest or the most gifted; He chooses those who will listen and obey. The lesson of the burning bush is not confined to a mountain in Midian; it is meant for us. The ground beneath our feet becomes holy when we recognize that God is present and active in our lives.

When God calls you to serve, don't focus on your inadequacy. Remember who is sending you. The "I AM" who empowered Moses still equips His people today. His promise remains the same: "I will certainly be with you." Trust that, and step forward in faith.

## Memory Verse and Weekly Challenge

*He answered, 'I will certainly be with you, and this will be the sign to you that I have sent you: when you bring the people out of Egypt, you will all worship God at this mountain.'"*
**Exodus 3:12 (CSB)**

God's assurance to Moses— "I will certainly be with you"—is the foundation of every calling. The same promise belongs to every believer who steps forward to serve in faith.

## Weekly Challenge

1. **Reflect on Your Own "Burning Bush" Moments.**

   Think about times when God may have been calling you to act, serve, or speak. Were you too busy, afraid, or uncertain to respond? This week, slow down and make space to listen.

2. **Serve in One Simple Way.**

   Look for one opportunity to serve someone in your daily routine—a word of encouragement, a visit, a prayer, or a helping hand. Let your ordinary moment become a place of holy service.

3. **Pray for Awareness.**

   Each morning, ask God to help you notice His presence in small things. Pray, "Lord, help me turn aside and see You today."

4. **Write Down Your Excuses.**

   Like Moses, we all have reasons to resist. List your main excuses, then write next to each one the words: *"God is with me."*

5. **Share a Testimony.**

   Before next class, tell someone how God is working in your life. It could be a story of how you served this week or how you sensed His presence in a moment of weakness.

# For Discussion

1. When you think about Moses' story, which part feels most like your own—being overlooked, feeling unqualified, or learning to trust God's presence?

   _____
   _____
   _____

2. How does the truth that *God reveals Himself before He sends us* change your view of service and ministry?

   _____
   _____
   _____

3. What are some ordinary places in your life where you could begin to see "holy ground"?

   _____
   _____
   _____

4. Why do you think God often calls people after long seasons of waiting or failure?

   _____
   _____
   _____

5. How can remembering "I will certainly be with you" strengthen your courage to obey God's call this week?

   _____
   _____
   _____

# Moses: Strength Made Perfect in Weakness

### Exodus 4:1–17

*But Moses replied to the Lord, "Please, Lord, I have never been eloquent—either in the past or recently, or since you have been speaking to your servant, because my mouth and my tongue are sluggish." The Lord said to him, "Who placed a mouth on humans? Who makes a person mute or deaf, seeing or blind? Is it not I, the Lord? Now go! I will help you speak and I will teach you what to say.*

### Exodus 4:10–12

**Class Overview:** After encountering God at the burning bush, Moses still struggled to believe he was the right person for the job. His doubts and fears mirror the same struggles we often face when God calls us to serve. In this lesson, we see how God patiently addressed Moses' excuses one by one, teaching that His strength is made perfect in human weakness. The Lord equips those who trust Him, not those who trust themselves. God's response to every excuse was the same: *"I will be with you."*

**Class Objectives:** By the end of this class, you should be able to—

1. Identify the excuses Moses used to resist God's call.
2. Understand how God's responses reveal His power and patience.
3. Recognize that weakness and fear do not disqualify a servant of God.
4. Apply the principle that God's power is displayed through obedience, not ability.
5. Commit to trusting God's sufficiency rather than personal strength in moments of calling or service.

# Introduction

MOSES STOOD BEFORE THE BURNING BUSH AND HEARD GOD'S VOICE, yet he still doubted himself. The task seemed impossible: confront Pharaoh, lead a nation, and speak on God's behalf. Moses had already failed once in Egypt. Now he was older, slower, and uncertain of his words. Fear crept in, and excuses followed. In Exodus 4, Moses gives one reason after another for why he cannot do what God commands. His story reminds us how quickly feelings of weakness can drown out faith.

Yet the beauty of this passage lies in God's response. The Lord does not scold Moses or abandon him. Instead, He patiently answers each objection, demonstrating that His power is more than enough to meet every need. When Moses worries about being believed, God provides signs. When Moses complains about his speech, God reminds him that the Creator of the mouth can give words. And when Moses begs to be excused, God sends Aaron to stand beside him. Through it all, God shows the same truth we must learn today: His strength is made perfect in weakness. The question is never whether we are able, it is whether we will trust the One who is.

## *Historical Background*

The conversation in Exodus 4 takes place on holy ground at Mount Horeb, a continuation of the events in chapter 3. Moses has already received his mission to return to Egypt, but he hesitates. At this time, Egypt was the world's most powerful empire, ruled by a Pharaoh who claimed divine authority. The Israelites had been enslaved for centuries, numbering in the hundreds of thousands. For Moses to go back and demand their freedom would have seemed suicidal. From a human perspective, his fear made sense.

But God was not sending Moses in his own power. The signs He gave, the staff turning into a snake, the leprous hand restored, and the water turned to blood, each demonstrated His authority over nature, disease, and even the gods of Egypt. These were not random miracles; they were previews of the plagues to come and proof that God alone was sovereign. Through these signs, Moses would learn that success depended not on persuasion or strength, but on obedience.

Moses' concern about his speech ("I am slow of speech and tongue") provides insight into how he sees himself. Some scholars believe he may have had a speech impediment, while others think he simply lacked confidence. Whatever the cause, God's response dismisses every excuse: "Who placed a mouth on humans? Who makes a person mute or deaf, seeing or blind? Is it not I, the Lord?" (Exodus 4:11). God reminds Moses that we do not limit the Creator of human abilities. The Lord's anger is stirred when Moses finally says, "Please, send someone else." Yet even then, God shows mercy by providing Aaron as a helper.

God's patience and power work together to shape His servants. He doesn't need perfect instruments—He perfects imperfect ones through His Spirit and providence. The same God who equipped Moses still meets His people in their weakness and enables them to serve His purpose with confidence and humility.

## God Is Patient with Our Weakness

When God called Moses, the conversation did not end with instant obedience. Moses hesitated, wrestling with self-doubt and fear. His words in Exodus 4:1 set the tone: *"What if they won't believe me and will not obey me but say, 'The Lord did not appear to you'?"* Beneath that question was a deeper struggle; Moses did not yet trust that God could work through him. The same man who had once acted rashly in Egypt now felt too broken to try again. Failure tends to silence confidence, and forty years in the desert had taught Moses how small he was. But God was not finished with him.

God's initial response reveals His patience. Instead of rebuking Moses, He offers reassurance through tangible signs. The staff turning into a snake, the hand becoming leprous and then restored, and the water turning to blood all showcase divine power. Each miracle addressed Moses' question of "what if." God was saying, "I will confirm My word. I will be with you. I will give evidence that this is not your doing but Mine." These signs were intended not only for Pharaoh and Israel but also for Moses himself. They served as visual reminders that God's presence transforms weakness into strength.

Moses' fear reflects the doubts many of us have when God calls us to serve. We ask, "What if they don't listen? What if I fail again? What if I'm not good enough?" But behind each question stands the same patient God, ready to meet us where we are. He does not expect perfection before obedience; He builds faith through obedience. God's patience with Moses shows His grace. He does not turn away the hesitant or fearful; He teaches them to trust.

Notice how personal God's approach is. He asks Moses to throw down his staff, the tool he uses daily as a shepherd. When it turns into a serpent and then back into a staff, God takes something ordinary and fills it with His power. The lesson is simple but powerful: when we surrender to God, the most common things in our hands can become tools for His purpose. What we see as insignificant, God can use greatly.

This patient training reveals the character of God. He is not only holy and mighty; He is kind and understanding. He knows our fears. Psalm 103:14 says, "He knows what we are made of, remembering that we are dust." God shapes servants slowly through questions, doubts, and small steps of faith. Even when Moses' faith wavered, God stayed near. Every objection brought new reassurance. Every weakness uncovered a fresh display of grace.

For us, the lesson is clear: God does not abandon reluctant servants. He keeps calling, equipping, and strengthening those who feel unworthy. The path of faith isn't about proving ourselves to God but about learning to trust His patience and power. When we offer Him our excuses, He responds with promises. When we present our fears, He responds with His presence. And when we show Him our weakness, He responds with grace.

Our service, then, should never be fueled by self-confidence but by trust in the One who calls. God is not looking for perfect people, He is looking for willing hearts. The story of Moses reminds us that the Lord who was patient with him is just as patient with us. If He could transform a hesitant shepherd into a bold deliverer, He can transform our uncertainty into courage. His patience is not an invitation to delay forever; it is a call to take the next step in faith.

# God Provides What We Lack

When Moses confessed, "Please, Lord, I have never been eloquent—either in the past or recently, or since you have been speaking to your servant" (Exodus 4:10), he revealed how deep his insecurity ran. He didn't deny God's power; he doubted his own usefulness. To Moses, leadership meant public speaking, persuasion, and authority; skills he didn't believe he had. But God saw the situation differently. What Moses viewed as a flaw, God saw as an opportunity to display His glory.

The Lord's answer cut through every excuse: "Who placed a mouth on humans? Who makes a person mute or deaf, seeing or blind? Is it not I, the Lord? Now go! I will help you speak and I will teach you what to say" (Exodus 4:11–12). God didn't deny Moses' weakness; He redefined it. The question wasn't whether Moses could speak, it was whether he believed God could work through him. This is where so many of God's people stumble. We focus on what we can't do, while God focuses on what He can do through us.

God's words remind us that He is the source of every ability we have. The One who formed our mouth knows how to fill it. The same truth applies to every area of service. The God who gives gifts also empowers their use. The moment we step forward in obedience, His strength meets us in our need. We may not feel prepared, but God promises His help: "I will teach you what to say." He does not hand us a script in advance; He walks with us in real time.

This pattern of divine provision appears throughout Scripture. Jeremiah told God, "I don't know how to speak," but the Lord touched his mouth and said, "I have put My words in your mouth" (Jeremiah 1:6–9). When Jesus sent out His disciples, He promised, "Don't worry about how or what you should speak... For the Holy Spirit will teach you at that very hour what must be said" (Luke 12:11–12). God equips His servants by giving them what they need, when they need it.

Moses' story also reminds us that feelings of inadequacy can be masked pride. When we insist we cannot serve because we lack ability, we are still making the work about ourselves. God calls us to shift the focus from *I can't* to *He can*. It's not about what we bring, it's about what we surrender. Weakness only becomes a barrier when we refuse to trust that God can supply what's missing.

God's provision goes beyond words. He offers strength to endure, courage to face challenges, wisdom for making decisions, and grace for every trial. For Moses, that provision even included a helper—his brother Aaron. God told him, "I know that he can speak well… You will speak with him and tell him what to say. I will help both you and him to speak" (Exodus 4:14–15). God didn't take away Moses' weakness; He surrounded it with support. His solution was not to make Moses self-sufficient but to make him dependent on divine help.

Every servant of God must learn this essential lesson. We are not self-sufficient vessels; we are vessels filled by the Spirit and strengthened by others. When God calls, He also equips, and His provision always fits the task. The strength of our ministry will never rely solely on personal talent or training, but on the living presence of God working through surrendered people.

This truth frees us from hesitation. We don't need to wait until we feel completely ready. We don't have to refine our speech or perfect our skills before serving. God's command remains: "Now go!" His presence is the assurance of success. Our job is not to be capable but to be available. The Lord who formed our mouths and shaped our lives knows exactly what He's doing when He calls us to serve. Our responsibility is simple: to trust His provision and obey His call.

## God Uses Imperfect Servants to Accomplish His Perfect Will

Even after witnessing miracles and hearing God's promises, Moses still hesitated. His final words in Exodus 4:13 are almost painful to read: *"Please, Lord, send someone else."* After every assurance and sign, Moses still wanted to step away. His fear had turned into outright resistance. But what stands out here is not only Moses' reluctance but also God's persistence. The Lord's anger burned, but His mercy remained. Instead of abandoning Moses, God changed His plan to include Aaron as his spokesman. This shows that God's purpose isn't dependent on perfect people. He accomplishes His will even through hesitant, fearful, and imperfect servants.

This moment reveals the tension between human weakness and divine sovereignty. Moses' fear was genuine, but God's mission would not fail. The Lord's plan was larger than Moses' comfort. He had chosen to deliver Israel, and He would use Moses, whether or not he felt prepared. This is one of the most encouraging truths in Scripture: God's faithfulness is not limited by our frailty. His work continues even when our faith falters. What matters most is not the perfection of the servant but the persistence of the God who calls.

In providing Aaron, God demonstrated both judgment and grace. Aaron's inclusion was a concession to Moses' fear, but it was also a blessing of partnership. The two brothers would stand before Pharaoh together, their combined service fulfilling God's will. This reminds us that God often uses community to strengthen the weak. He rarely sends us alone. He surrounds us with others who complement our strengths and balance our weaknesses. In doing so, He teaches humility and dependence, not on us, but on Him and one another.

Throughout the rest of Moses's life, the same truth kept unfolding. His flaws never went away. He struggled with frustration, anger, and doubt. Yet, through it all, God worked powerfully through him. He confronted Pharaoh, led Israel through the sea, and received the Law on Sinai. The man who once said, "Please, send someone else," became the one through whom God showed His power to an entire nation. This change didn't happen because Moses changed himself — it happened because God never gave up on him.

That same persistence defines God's relationship with us. He does not discard those who hesitate or stumble. Instead, He shapes them through experience, correction, and grace. The apostle Paul later expressed this truth when he wrote, "We have this treasure in clay jars, so that this extraordinary power may be from God and not from us" (2 Corinthians 4:7). Our weakness highlights His strength. Our inadequacy magnifies His sufficiency. God's purpose is to display His glory through broken vessels that rely on Him completely.

This should bring us both humility and hope. It humbles us because we realize that none of us serves from a place of perfection. Every preacher, teacher, and servant of God carries flaws. But it also offers hope because God delights in using those flaws as part of His plan. If He waited for perfect people, nothing would ever be accomplished. Instead, He refines and repurposes imperfect ones. Like Moses, we may hesitate, fear, or falter, but God's grace keeps working until His will is fulfilled.

The lesson concludes where it started; with the assurance of God's presence. Even when Moses doubted and hesitated, God never took back His promise: "I will be with you." That truth carried Moses through Pharaoh's court, across the Red Sea, and through forty more years of hardship. It can also carry us. God's strength isn't based on perfect servants; it rests on perfect faithfulness. And that faithfulness has never failed.

## Lesson Summary and Reflection

The story of Moses at the burning bush continues in Exodus 4 with a conversation that resembles our own prayers: full of fear, excuses, and hesitation. God had called, but Moses couldn't see past his weakness. He worried that no one would believe him, that he lacked the skills to speak, and that someone else would be better suited for the task. Yet, through every objection, God patiently revealed His power and His purpose. The lesson is not about Moses' confidence growing stronger, but about his dependence on God becoming deeper.

*God's patience* is one of the most comforting truths in this passage. He did not give up when Moses questioned Him. Instead, He provided Moses with signs to strengthen his faith, words to speak, and a helper in Aaron. Each act of grace shows that God does not demand instant perfection from His servants—He develops faith gradually. His patience reminds us that He understands our weaknesses, but He will not let those weaknesses have the final say.

We also see that *God provides exactly what His people need for the work He calls them to do.* Moses said, "I can't speak," but God replied, "I made your mouth." That exchange captures the heart of service. God does not ask us to serve from our strength but from His. Whatever He requires, He provides—whether wisdom, courage, opportunity, or support from others. The calling of God is always matched by the enabling of God.

The third major lesson from this story is that *God's plan does not fail because His servants are imperfect.* Moses was hesitant and afraid, yet God used him to stand before Pharaoh and lead Israel to freedom. The success of the mission depended on God's faithfulness, not Moses' performance. That same truth supports every believer today. We are not expected to be perfect instruments, only willing ones. God works through weakness so that His strength may be shown.

When we assemble all of this, the message is clear: God's strength is made perfect in weakness. He calls ordinary, unsure people and fills them with His power. Our job is not to prove ourselves, but to trust Him. If God could transform a hesitant shepherd into a great deliverer, He can use anyone who is willing to say, "Here I am."

### Key Truths

- God is patient with those who doubt or fear His calling.
- Every weakness becomes an opportunity for God to display His strength.
- The Lord provides everything His servants need to obey.
- God's plans are not hindered by human imperfection.
- True service flows from trust, not self-confidence.

# Conclusion

God is not limited by what restricts us. He uses hesitant hearts, weak voices, and trembling hands to fulfill His will. The same God who called Moses calls us today to serve. He still responds to every excuse with the same promise: "I will be with you."

When you feel unqualified, remember that Moses felt the same way. When you fear failure, remember that God's power surpasses your fears. The Lord who formed your mouth, your mind, and your life knows exactly what He's doing. All He asks is that you trust Him enough to take the next step.

# Memory Verse and Weekly Challenge

*Now go! I will help you speak and I will teach you what to say.*
**Exodus 4:12 (CSB)**

Here we see God's promise to every servant who feels unqualified. It shifts the focus from what we lack to what God supplies. When He calls, He equips. When He sends, He goes with us.

**Weekly Challenge**

1. **Face One Fear.**
   Identify one area where fear or self-doubt has kept you from serving. Pray over it this week and take one small, concrete step of obedience.

2. **Use What's in Your Hand.**
   Moses' staff was a simple shepherd's tool, yet God used it powerfully. Ask yourself, *What has God already placed in my hand?* Use it for His glory this week—whether time, talent, or opportunity.

3. **Memorize and Pray Exodus 4:12.**
   Begin each morning repeating this verse as a prayer: "Lord, help me speak and teach me what to say."

4. **Encourage Another Servant.**
   Look for someone in the church who feels uncertain about their role. Encourage them with the same truth God gave Moses: *You are not alone—God is with you.*

5. **Reflect on God's Patience.**
   Spend time in prayer thanking God for His patience with you. Ask Him to replace your hesitation with trust and your weakness with faith.

# For Discussion

1. Which of Moses' excuses in Exodus 4 do you most identify with—
   and why?

   _____

   _____

   _____

2. How has God shown patience with your weakness in the past?

   _____

   _____

   _____

3. What are some practical ways to rely on God's provision instead of
   your own ability when serving?

   _____

   _____

   _____

4. How does God's use of Aaron to help Moses illustrate the
   importance of working together in ministry?

   _____

   _____

   _____

5. What step of faith is God asking you to take right now, even though
   you don't feel ready?

   _____

   _____

   _____

# Joshua:
# Courage for the Task

## Joshua 1:1–9

*Haven't I commanded you: be strong and courageous? Do not be afraid or discouraged, for the Lord your God is with you wherever you go.*
**Joshua 1:9**

**Class Overview:** After Moses' death, the weight of leadership fell upon Joshua. The wilderness generation was gone, and the time had come for Israel to cross the Jordan and claim the land God had promised. Joshua faced overwhelming responsibility, a grieving nation, and a future filled with uncertainty. Yet God's message to him was clear and repeated three times: *"Be strong and courageous."* This lesson shows that courage in God's service is not the absence of fear but the presence of faith. The same God who strengthened Joshua to lead Israel gives His people courage today to obey His word and trust His promises.

**Class Objectives:**

By the end of this class, you should be able to:

1. Understand the historical and spiritual transition from Moses to Joshua.
2. Explain what true courage looks like in the context of faith and obedience.
3. Identify the promises God gave Joshua and how they apply to believers today.
4. Recognize that courage grows from confidence in God's presence and word.
5. Commit to taking courageous steps of obedience in your own walk with God.

# Introduction

JOSHUA'S STORY BEGINS AT A CRUCIAL, DIFFICULT MOMENT in Israel's history. Moses, the only leader the people had ever known, was gone. The wilderness wanderings had ended, and the next step was to enter the land of Canaan: a place filled with fortified cities, mighty armies, and long-standing enemies. For forty years, Joshua had served as Moses' assistant, standing faithfully by his side. But now, the responsibility was fully on his shoulders. The future of a nation depended on his leadership and bravery.

It's not surprising that Joshua felt overwhelmed by fear. The people depended on him for strength, yet he was mourning the loss of his mentor. The road ahead would test every bit of his faith. That's why God spoke to him so clearly and repeatedly: "Be strong and courageous." These words were divine commands based on a promise. Joshua's courage wouldn't come from personality or experience alone but from the certainty that God was with him.

The lesson of Joshua 1:1–9 speaks for all time. Each generation of God's people faces its own moments of change, challenge, and uncertainty. Whether stepping into a new role, enduring hardship, or standing for truth, the message remains the same: be strong and courageous. True courage isn't the absence of fear but the choice to trust God's presence and follow His word despite fear. Joshua's story shows that strength for the task always comes from the One who sends us.

## *Historical Background*

Joshua was familiar with leadership and battle. His name means "The Lord is salvation," and he had long served as Moses' trusted follower. He led Israel's forces against Amalek (Exodus 17), accompanied Moses partway up Mount Sinai (Exodus 24), and was one of the twelve spies who surveyed the Promised Land (Numbers 13). Along with Caleb, he believed in God's promise and encouraged the people to enter the land forty years earlier. Because of his faith, he and Caleb were the only two of their generation allowed to see Canaan.

By the time of Joshua 1, the nation had spent forty years wandering in the wilderness. Moses had died on Mount Nebo, and God had buried him there (Deuteronomy 34:5–6). Israel was camped on the plains of Moab, across the Jordan River from Jericho. The people were tired but hopeful. They had seen God's power in the wilderness, but now they faced a new kind of challenge: settling and securing the land. The task was humanly impossible, yet God's promise was sure: "Every place the sole of your foot treads, I have given to you" (Joshua 1:3).

The command "Be strong and courageous" appears three times in this chapter (vv. 6, 7, 9), each linked to a specific reason. Joshua was to be strong because of God's *promise* ("You will distribute the land I swore to their ancestors"), strong through God's *word* ("Be careful to observe everything written in it"), and strong in God's *presence* ("The Lord your God is with you wherever you go"). These three truths form the foundation of all courage in serving God.

Joshua's mission was clear: lead the people into the land and follow the Book of the Law. Israel's success wouldn't rely on military power but on spiritual obedience. Just as God had been with Moses, He now promised to be with Joshua. That reassurance turned fear into faith and gave him the courage to face every battle ahead.

## God's Promises Bring Courage

The first words Joshua heard after Moses' death were filled with both grief and hope: *"Moses my servant is dead. Now you and all the people prepare to cross over the Jordan to the land I am giving the Israelites"* (Joshua 1:2). Joshua had lost his mentor and friend, but the work of God was not over. The promises of God did not die with Moses. What God had spoken to Abraham, Isaac, and Jacob centuries earlier was still certain. God's plan never depends on one person; it continues through every generation that trusts Him.

God grounded Joshua's courage in His promises. He said, *"Every place the sole of your foot treads, I have given to you ... No one will be able to stand against you as long as you live. I will be with you, just as I was with Moses. I will not leave you or abandon you"* (Joshua 1:3–5). Before Joshua lifted a sword or crossed a river, God reminded him that victory was already secured. The land was described in the past tense, *"I have given you,"* because in God's mind, the outcome was already decided. Courage grows when we believe that God's promises are stronger than our problems.

These promises were not vague assurances; they were specific and based on history. God had sworn to Abraham that his descendants would inherit the land (Genesis 12:7; 15:18). Now that promise was coming true through Joshua. The same God who had parted the Red Sea was about to part the Jordan. The same God who had fed Israel in the wilderness would now fight for them in Canaan. Joshua could face the future with confidence, not because he was experienced, but because God was faithful.

The command to "be strong and courageous" in verse 6 is based on that foundation. God linked Joshua's strength to His faithfulness: *"For you will distribute the land I swore to their ancestors to give them."* The word *swore* is essential. God commits Himself to His word. What He promises, He fulfills. Joshua's courage didn't come from optimism or self-confidence. It came from knowing that the God who called him could not lie.

This truth still applies to God's people today. We find courage in the promises of His word. When Jesus said, "I am with you always," He offered the same assurance Joshua received. When He said, "I will build my church," He proclaimed that His plans would endure despite opposition. Every act of obedience we undertake is built on a foundation of divine certainty. We can move forward into unknown territory because God has already gone ahead of us.

Practical faith starts when we stop judging challenges by their size and begin judging them by God's faithfulness. Fear often grows in the space where promises are forgotten. That's why God began with reassurance: *"I will not leave you or abandon you."* The strength to lead, teach, or serve doesn't come from what we can control, it comes from recalling what God has already said.

When we anchor our hearts in His promises, courage comes naturally. We can face grief, uncertainty, and overwhelming tasks with peace because the same God who stood beside Joshua stands with us. The command "Be strong and courageous" isn't about self-confidence; it's a call to trust in the unchanging faithfulness of God.

## God's Word Sustains Courage

After reminding Joshua of His promises, God gave him another source of strength: His Word. *"Be strong and very courageous to observe carefully the whole instruction my servant Moses commanded you. Do not turn from it to the right or the left, so that you will have success wherever you go. This book of instruction must not depart from your mouth; you are to meditate on it day and night so that you may carefully observe everything written in it. For then you will prosper and succeed in whatever you do"* (Joshua 1:7–8).

Courage is not just emotional; it is moral and spiritual. Joshua's success relied not on clever strategy or military power but on faithful obedience to God's revealed will. God did not instruct him to study the enemy's defenses; He commanded him to study His Word. True strength comes from knowing, trusting, and applying what God has spoken.

God told Joshua to keep His Word on his lips, in his mind, and in his actions. Each phrase holds importance. "Do not let it depart from your mouth" means speak it often: teach it, discuss it, and encourage others with it. "Meditate on it day and night" means let it fill your thoughts continuously. Courage grows when Scripture influences how we see the world. "Observe everything written in it" means obedience must be complete, not selective. Joshua could not follow God halfway or only when it was convenient. Every decision, battle plan, and command must come from God's Word.

This pattern is vital for everyone who serves God today. The more we understand His Word, the more we trust His promises. Scripture trains the heart to overcome fear by keeping us focused on God's truth rather than our circumstances. Psalm 1 describes the person who delights in the Lord's instruction and meditates on it day and night as being "like a tree planted beside flowing streams." Strength and stability come from deep roots in God's Word.

Courage without Scripture quickly turns to presumption. Israel's later defeats during Joshua's lifetime (such as at Ai in chapter 7) show that success without obedience is impossible. God wanted Joshua to realize that His presence and blessing would stay only as long as His Word remained the focus. The same principle applies to the church. We can develop programs, train leaders, and plan strategies, but without Scripture as the foundation, spiritual strength diminishes.

To "not turn from it to the right or the left" means staying true when pressures pull in all directions. Courageous faith remains steady even when it's unpopular or costly. For Joshua, that involved trusting God's commands even when the plan seemed impossible, like marching around Jericho's walls in silence. For us, it means living by God's truth when culture, convenience, or comfort urge us to compromise.

God's call to meditate day and night challenges us to let Scripture do more than inform—it must transform. Reading the Word fuels courage; obeying it completes it. We don't need to summon bravery from within; we need to stay close to the voice that gives it. The same Spirit who strengthened Joshua strengthens us through the Word today. When God's Word fills our hearts, His courage fills our lives.

In short, Joshua's courage did not stem from pep talks or positive thinking. It came from a steady, disciplined walk with God through His Word. Strength diminishes when we drift away from Scripture; it grows when we stay in it. As God told Joshua, success and peace belong to those who keep His Word at the center of their lives.

## God's Presence Empowers Courage

After reminding Joshua of His promises and instructing him to remain grounded in His Word, God provided one final source of courage: His constant presence. Verse 9 highlights this message best: *"Haven't I commanded you: be strong and courageous? Do not be afraid or discouraged, for the Lord your God is with you wherever you go."*

This wasn't a new idea for Joshua. He had experienced God's presence through Moses for many years. He had stood at the base of Mount Sinai, where God's glory appeared in fire and cloud. He had watched the pillar of cloud by day and the pillar of fire by night leading the people. But now, the assurance was personal. The same divine presence that once rested on Moses would now be with him. Joshua wouldn't be leading alone.

Fear and discouragement are natural during moments of great responsibility. Joshua faced the huge challenge of leading a nation into uncharted territory and capturing fortified cities. Still, God didn't provide him with detailed battle plans or maps. He gave him Himself. That truth is what makes biblical courage different from human bravery. Human courage depends on preparation and confidence; divine courage depends on God's presence.

Throughout Scripture, God's presence is consistently the answer to fear. When He called Moses, He said, "I will be with you" (Exodus 3:12). When Gideon hesitated, He said, "Go in the strength you have … I will be with you" (Judges 6:14–16). When Jesus sent His disciples into the world, His final words were, "I am with you always" (Matthew 28:20). The pattern remains the same: God's presence is His greatest gift to His followers.

Notice that in verse 9, God repeats his command to Joshua: "Do not be afraid" and "Do not be discouraged." These two phrases address the main enemies of faith. Fear looks ahead and imagines defeat, while discouragement looks back and dwells on failure. Both steal courage. The remedy for both is the same, remembering that the Lord is near. Courage does not mean we stop feeling afraid; it means we choose to act in faith rather than fear, because we know God is with us.

For Christians today, the promise of God's presence feels even more personal. Through the Holy Spirit, God lives within us. We don't just have God beside us, we carry His power inside. That presence provides comfort in hardships, guidance when we're confused, and strength when we are weak. When we feel lonely or overwhelmed, we can echo David's words: "Even when I go through the darkest valley, I fear no danger, for You are with me" (Psalm 23:4).

The greatest challenge to Joshua's courage would come later, as he faced opposition, disobedience among his own people, and years of warfare.

Yet each victory came from one unwavering truth: God was with him. The same applies to us. Our strength for service, our endurance through trials, and our confidence in the face of fear all depend on this promise.

When God said, "The Lord your God is with you wherever you go," He eliminated every condition. His presence is constant, whether in victory or failure, in peace or conflict. That promise allows us to serve boldly and faithfully. We might not know the future, but we know who goes with us into it. *The courage to do God's will doesn't come from who we are or what we can do—it comes from the God who never leaves us.*

## Lesson Summary and Reflection

Joshua 1 marks a pivotal moment in Israel's history. With Moses gone, Joshua must lead the next generation into God's promises. The task is daunting, the people are anxious, and the future is uncertain. But God speaks to Joshua with words that resonate with every servant who has ever faced fear: *"Be strong and courageous."* Those words are not just encouragement. They are a command based on three powerful truths. God's promises inspire courage, His Word sustains courage, and His presence empowers courage.

First, *courage starts with trusting in God's promises.* The Lord reminded Joshua that His plan had not failed. What He swore to Abraham centuries earlier remains certain. The land has already been given, and victory is already assured. Joshua could move forward confidently because God's word is dependable. The same truth applies to us. When we rely on God's promises, fear loses its strength. His faithfulness surpasses any obstacle we face.

Second, *courage is upheld by Scripture.* God instructed Joshua to keep His Word constantly in his mind—to speak it, meditate on it, and obey it fully. The command to "not turn from it to the right or to the left" reminds us that courage and obedience are inseparable. The person who lives by God's Word will not break down under pressure. When God's truth fills our thoughts, our outlook shifts. We stop listening to fear and start listening to faith.

Finally, *courage is strengthened by God's presence.* "Do not be afraid or discouraged," God said, "for the Lord your God is with you wherever you go." That promise was enough for Joshua, and it is enough for us. God never leaves His people alone. His presence transforms impossible tasks into opportunities for faith. When we know He is near, fear no longer controls us.

Strength and courage come from trust, not talent. We find courage when we remember that God keeps His promises, guides us through His Word, and walks with us in every situation. The same God who called Joshua to lead His people into the Promised Land calls us to live boldly in His service today. He still says, "Be strong and courageous... I will be with you wherever you go."

### Key Truths

- God's promises are the foundation of lasting courage.
- Scripture strengthens faith and guards against fear.
- True courage means trusting and obeying God, even when afraid.
- God's presence removes the need to rely on our own strength.
- Every challenge becomes an opportunity to prove God's faithfulness.

# Conclusion

Joshua's courage did not come from himself; it was rooted in God. Every victory he won, every battle he faced, started with faith in God's presence and promise. The same holds true for us today. The call to "be strong and courageous" isn't about ignoring fear but overcoming it through faith. God has already provided us with everything we need for life and godliness (2 Peter 1:3). The question is whether we will trust Him enough to act.

When you face a moment of uncertainty or transition, remember Joshua's lesson. Stand on God's promises. Stay grounded in His Word. Trust His presence. The Lord who was with Joshua is with you. And with Him beside you, there is no reason to fear the task ahead.

# Memory Verse and Weekly Challenge

*Haven't I commanded you: be strong and courageous? Do not be afraid
or discouraged, for the Lord your God is with you wherever you go.*
**Joshua 1:9 (CSB)**

This verse captures the heart of Joshua's call and the foundation of all
Christian courage. It reminds us that fear fades when we remember who
walks beside us. God's presence is not occasional—it is constant.

**Weekly Challenge**

1. **Memorize Joshua 1:9.**
   Repeat it daily until it becomes part of your thinking. Let it remind
   you that courage is not self-made—it's God-given.

2. **Face One Fear with Faith.**
   Identify a situation where fear or hesitation has held you back. Pray
   specifically for courage to obey God in that area this week.

3. **Read God's Word Daily.**
   Follow God's command to Joshua by setting aside time each day to
   meditate on Scripture. Ask, "What is God teaching me through His
   Word today?"

4. **Encourage Another Believer.**
   Find someone who feels discouraged or uncertain. Share Joshua 1:9
   with them and remind them that God is with them, too.

5. **Record a Victory.**
   At the end of the week, write down one way God gave you courage
   to act when you felt afraid. Use it as a personal testimony of His
   faithfulness.

# For Discussion

1. What fears or uncertainties are keeping you from stepping into something God is calling you to do?

   _____

   _____

   _____

2. Which of God's promises gives you the most courage when life feels overwhelming?

   _____

   _____

   _____

3. How can you keep God's Word at the center of your thoughts and decisions this week?

   _____

   _____

   _____

4. In what ways have you experienced the truth of God's presence during difficult times?

   _____

   _____

   _____

5. How can Joshua's example help you lead, serve, or stand firm when others are hesitant or afraid?

   _____

   _____

   _____

# Gideon:
# God's Power in Our Weakness
### Judges 6:11–24

*The Lord turned to him and said, "Go in the strength you have and deliver Israel from the grasp of Midian. I am sending you!"*
**Judges 6:14**

**Class Overview:** Gideon's story begins in a season of fear and oppression. Israel had turned from God, and the Midianites were devastating the land. When God called Gideon to deliver His people, Gideon was hiding in a winepress, threshing wheat in secret. He saw himself as the least in his family and his family as the weakest in Israel. Yet God called him a "valiant warrior." This lesson shows how God's power shines through human weakness. The Lord does not choose people because of their strength; He makes them strong because of His presence. Gideon's call reminds us that God delights in using ordinary people who trust Him completely.

**Class Objectives:** By the end of this class, you should be able to—

1. Describe the spiritual and historical background of Israel during Gideon's time.
2. Understand how God's call transforms fear into faith.
3. Explain the meaning of the angel's words, "The Lord is with you, valiant warrior."
4. Recognize that God's power is displayed most clearly through human weakness.
5. Commit to trusting God's strength rather than your own ability when facing challenges.

# Introduction

WHEN THE ANGEL OF THE LORD FIRST APPEARED TO GIDEON, he was not leading an army or standing on a battlefield—he was hiding. The Midianites had overrun Israel, destroying crops and livestock, leaving the people in fear and poverty. Gideon was threshing wheat in a winepress, trying to stay out of sight. He felt insignificant, weak, and forgotten. Yet in that unlikely moment, God called him a *"valiant warrior."* Those words must have sounded absurd to a man hiding from his enemies, but they reveal how God sees differently than we do.

The story of Gideon shows how God takes fearful people and transforms them into faithful servants. When God called Gideon to save Israel, Gideon listed his weaknesses. His family was poor, his tribe was small, and he lacked confidence. But God responded to every doubt with one promise: *"I will be with you."* That same promise gave Gideon the courage to face his fears and shaped him into the leader God intended. Our true measure of strength isn't what we bring to God, but what God brings to us. When He calls us, He also gives us the strength we need.

## *Historical Background*

The book of Judges outlines one of the darkest periods in Israel's history. After Joshua's death, the people turned away from God and started worshiping Canaanite idols. This led to a recurring pattern: sin, oppression, repentance, and deliverance. Each time Israel cried out for help, God raised up a deliverer, or judge, to save them. Gideon was one of those judges.

By the time of Judges 6, Israel had been under oppression by the Midianites for seven years. The Midianites were desert raiders who invaded Israel every harvest season, destroying crops and livestock. The people were forced to live in caves and strongholds to survive. The oppression was so harsh that Israel finally cried out to God for help. Before sending Gideon, God sent a prophet to remind the people why they were suffering — it was their own unfaithfulness that had made them vulnerable to Midian's power.

Against this bleak backdrop, the angel of the Lord appeared to Gideon at Ophrah. The setting is full of irony: Gideon was threshing wheat in a winepress, a small pit usually used for crushing grapes. He was doing the right work in the wrong place—trying to feed his family while hiding from the enemy. Into that fear-filled scene, the angel declared, *"The Lord is with you, valiant warrior."* Gideon could not see himself that way, but God saw what he could become.

Gideon's call took place around the 12th century B.C., during a period of intense spiritual decline. Israel had forgotten the God who delivered them from Egypt. Yet even amid their rebellion, God's grace remained. He came not to destroy Gideon's weakness but to transform it. The altar Gideon built after this encounter was called *The Lord Is Peace*—a sign that God had met him in fear and replaced it with confidence. From that moment on, Gideon's story became a testimony that God's power is perfected in weakness.

## God Meets Us in Our Fear

When the angel of the Lord found Gideon, he wasn't standing tall in faith; he was crouched low in fear. Judges 6:11 says he was *"threshing wheat in the winepress in order to hide it from the Midianites."* Typically, threshing was done on a hilltop so the wind could separate grain from chaff. But Gideon was doing it in a pit, where no one could see him. That single detail captures Israel's condition: defeated, discouraged, and afraid. It also shows how God works. He meets His servants where they are, not where they wish they were.

The angel's greeting seemed entirely out of place: *"The Lord is with you, valiant warrior."* (Judges 6:12). Gideon must have looked around to see who the angel was talking to. Nothing about his situation appeared heroic. Yet God called him not for what he was, but for what he could become through faith. This is how God always works. He sees potential where we see problems. He recognizes strength where we see weakness. He names us according to His purpose, not our fears.

Gideon's initial reaction was doubt: *"If the Lord is with us, why has all this happened to us?"* (v. 13). His words show both confusion and disappointment. He had heard stories of God's power before, how the Lord led Israel out of Egypt, but he couldn't reconcile those memories with his current suffering. Like many of us, Gideon believed God had worked in the past, but he found it hard to believe He was still active now. Yet even in his doubt, God didn't rebuke him. Instead, He turned to him and said, *"Go in the strength you have and deliver Israel… I am sending you!"* (v. 14).

God doesn't wait for us to overcome fear before calling us. He calls us while we are afraid and provides strength as we move forward. God didn't promise Gideon comfort; He promised His presence. "I am sending you," He said, reminding Gideon that the mission wasn't based on personal ability but divine authority. The same principle applies today. Our calling isn't about what we can manage, but about what God can do through us when we obey.

Also notice the tenderness of God's patience. Gideon's response was still hesitant: *"Please, Lord, how can I deliver Israel? My family is the weakest in Manasseh, and I am the youngest in my father's family"* (v. 15). Every line of that protest is shaped by fear and insecurity. But God answered again, *"But I will be with you. You will strike Midian down as if it were one man."* (v. 16). Those words echo the same assurance given to Moses, Joshua, and every servant God has ever called: *"I will be with you."* That promise is the cure for fear.

Courage doesn't come from pretending we're fearless, it comes from trusting that God is near. Gideon's circumstances hadn't changed when God spoke, but his confidence began to grow because he realized he wasn't alone. God's presence transforms hidden people into courageous ones.

Every Christian can relate to Gideon's experience in the winepress. We all understand what it's like to feel overwhelmed or inadequate. But God still finds us there. He doesn't wait for us to get out; He steps into our fear and speaks peace into our hearts. His call always begins with grace. "The Lord is with you." That truth alone gives us strength to rise, obey, and trust that His power is greater than our fear.

# God's Presence Turns Weakness into Strength

When Gideon finally realized who was speaking to him, his fear deepened before it lifted. The angel of the Lord had told him, *"Go in the strength you have,"* but Gideon couldn't see any strength at all. He protested, *"My family is the weakest in Manasseh, and I am the youngest in my father's family"* (Judges 6:15). Everything about his situation screamed inadequacy. He saw himself as powerless, small, and unqualified. Yet that was exactly the kind of person God was looking for.

God's reply arrived with unwavering certainty: *"But I will be with you. You will strike Midian down as if it were one man"* (v. 16). That single promise changed everything. The success of the mission would not rely on Gideon's strength but on God's presence. The Lord did not dismiss Gideon's weakness; *He redefined it.* Gideon saw weakness as a barrier; God saw it as the very place where His power could be displayed.

We see this throughout Scripture. When Moses said, "I am slow of speech," God replied, "I made your mouth." When Jeremiah said, "I don't know how to speak," God answered, "I have put My words in your mouth." When Paul pleaded for his thorn to be taken away, the Lord said, "My grace is sufficient for you, for My power is perfected in weakness." God never chooses people because they are strong; He chooses them so that His strength can be seen through their weakness.

For Gideon, the turning point was learning to trust that *God's presence is powerful enough.* When the Lord said, "Go in the strength you have," He wasn't suggesting Gideon had hidden potential inside him; He was reminding Gideon that divine strength was already with him. God was not asking him to act out of self-confidence but out of faith. Courage is born the moment we stop focusing on what we lack and start believing Who is beside us.

In verse 17, Gideon asked for a sign, not to test God's patience but to confirm His promise. He brought an offering, a young goat and unleavened bread, and laid it on a rock. The angel touched it with the tip of his staff, and fire shot out from the rock, consuming the sacrifice. It served as a vivid reminder that God's power was real and present. Gideon fell in fear, realizing he had seen the angel of the Lord face to face. But instead of judgment, God offered peace: *"Peace to you. Don't be afraid, for you will not die"* (v. 23).

That peace became the foundation of Gideon's courage. He built an altar and named it *The Lord Is Peace.* Before leading an army or sounding a trumpet, Gideon learned the most important lesson of all: peace with God must come before victory for God. When we experience His presence, fear loses its grip. The God who met Gideon in fear now met him in peace, transforming a frightened man into a faithful warrior.

This same truth still strengthens believers today. God's presence transforms weakness. We often want to wait until we feel strong or ready before serving, but strength comes after obedience, not before. When God calls us, He doesn't give us a list of qualifications, *He gives us Himself.* His Spirit, His Word, and His promises become the resources we need. As Paul later wrote, "We have this treasure in clay jars, so that this extraordinary power may be from God and not from us."

In Gideon's life, the story of transformation started in a winepress and moved to an altar. The place of fear became a place of peace. The man who once hid from the enemy would soon face them with faith. And the only difference was this: God was with him. That same assurance is enough for us. No matter what weakness we bring, His presence is greater. God never asks for strength, only trust.

## God Confirms His Call to Strengthen Our Faith

Even after hearing God's promise and witnessing fire consume his offering, Gideon continued to doubt. Fear doesn't disappear instantly; it diminishes as faith grows. Gideon believed, but he still needed reassurance. What stands out in his story is how patient God remained. The Lord didn't scold him for seeking confirmation; instead, He steadily strengthened his faith.

Later in Judges 6, Gideon requested a sign involving a wool fleece and the morning dew. He said, *"If you will deliver Israel by my hand, as You said, I will place a wool fleece on the threshing floor. If dew is only on the fleece and the ground remains dry, I will know that You will deliver Israel through my strength, as You promised."* When he woke up the next morning, the fleece was soaked, but the ground was dry. Still uncertain, Gideon asked again—this time for the opposite result. Once more, God answered. He responded to Gideon's fragile faith with patient reassurance.

Many have criticized Gideon for these requests, but his motive was not rebellion, it was insecurity. He wanted to be sure that it was truly God's voice calling him to such a dangerous task. In his weakness, he sought confirmation, and God graciously provided it. The lesson is not to imitate Gideon's method but to appreciate God's mercy. The Lord understands our hesitations and meets us where our faith wavers.

God's patient reassurance remains constant throughout Scripture. God showed Moses miraculous signs, Joshua a visible commander of His army, and Thomas the chance to touch the risen Christ's hands. Faith doesn't mean never needing encouragement; it means bringing our questions to God rather than running from Him. Gideon's honesty became the doorway to deeper trust. Each sign boosted his confidence, preparing him for the battle ahead.

The true miracle in this part of Gideon's story isn't the fleece; it's the change in his heart. When God first spoke to him, Gideon focused on his weakness and Israel's defeat. Now, after experiencing God's presence and power, his focus shifts to obedience. When the Lord later told him to tear down his father's altar to Baal, Gideon obeyed, even though he was scared. That act of obedience marked a turning point. Fear still existed, but faith was starting to lead.

Our faith develops gradually. God often confirms His call through His Word, answered prayers, open doors, or the encouragement of others. Each confirmation is meant to propel us forward, not keep us stuck in doubt. God's goal isn't to eliminate all risk but to deepen our trust. Courage arises as we take one step at a time, witnessing His faithfulness along the way.

For Christians today, Gideon's story reminds us that God's patience and presence remain constant, even when our faith falters. He does not scorn small beginnings or hesitant obedience. When we take the next step, even with trembling hands, He meets us with strength. As Psalm 103:13–14 says, *"As a father has compassion on his children, so the Lord has compassion on those who fear Him. For He knows what we are made of, remembering that we are dust."*

God's call is never meant to crush us; it is intended to shape us. He confirms it to remind us that we are not alone and that His strength will be enough. Gideon started as a fearful man hiding in a pit, but God patiently built his faith until he could stand as a leader, confident not in himself but in the Lord. That same God still calls us to step out, trust Him, and let His power be made perfect in our weakness.

## Lesson Summary and Reflection

The story of Gideon shows us that God's power shines brightest when His people feel weakest. When the angel of the Lord found Gideon, he was hiding in fear. Yet God called him a "valiant warrior" and sent him to deliver Israel from Midian. That call seemed impossible, but it revealed a timeless truth: God does not wait for strength—He supplies it. What matters most is not our confidence but His presence.

Gideon learned three key lessons. First, *God meets us in our fear.* The Lord didn't wait for Gideon to find courage; He came to him while he was hiding. He spoke peace to a frightened man and gave him a new identity. God still does the same today. He calls us not for who we are, but for what His grace can transform us into.

Second, *God's presence turns weakness into strength.* When Gideon said, "My family is the weakest," God answered, "I will be with you." That promise transformed the whole situation. Victory would not depend on Gideon's ability but on God's power. The consuming fire on the altar proved that divine strength was already at work. Gideon named that place *The Lord Is Peace*—the moment fear began to give way to faith.

Third, *God affirms His call to strengthen our faith.* Gideon's repeated need for reassurance did not turn God away—it revealed His patience. The Lord responded to Gideon's vulnerable faith with grace, giving signs that increased his trust and prepared him for obedience. God understands our hesitations. He builds confidence over time through His Word, His presence, and His faithfulness.

The story of Gideon isn't about a hero who finds courage, it's about a God who gives courage to those who trust Him. Gideon's journey from hiding in a winepress to leading an army began with one truth: "The Lord is with you." That same promise still stands for us. When we bring our fears and weaknesses to Him, He transforms them into tools for victory. His strength is perfected in our weakness.

**Key Truths**

- God meets His people in their fear, not after they overcome it.
- The presence of God is the source of real strength.
- Weakness is not a barrier to service—it's the doorway for God's power.
- God patiently confirms His call and strengthens our faith step by step.
- Peace with God gives courage to face any battle for God.

# Conclusion

Gideon's story proves that God can use anyone willing to trust Him. He turns hiding spots into sacred ground and fearful hearts into faithful ones. Every excuse Gideon made was met with a promise: "I will be with you." That truth has never changed.

You may feel weak, unqualified, or afraid. But God's call doesn't depend on your strength. It depends on His. He remains the Lord of peace, remains patient with doubters, and remains powerful through the humble. When He calls you to act, go with the strength you have. He will provide what you lack, confirm what He commands, and accomplish His will through your faith.

# Memory Verse and Weekly Challenge

*The Lord turned to him and said, "Go in the strength you have and deliver Israel from the grasp of Midian. I am sending you!"*
**Judges 6:14 (CSB)**

This verse captures the message of Gideon's call. God did not tell him to become stronger before obeying, He told him to go in the strength already given, trusting that His presence would supply the rest. The same command calls every Christian today to move forward in faith, even when confidence feels small.

**Weekly Challenge**

1. **Identify Your "Winepress."**
   Reflect on an area of life where fear has made you hide: an opportunity avoided, a conversation delayed, or a step of faith resisted. This week, ask God for courage to face it.

2. **Remember God's Presence.**
   Write the phrase *"I will be with you"* somewhere visible—on your desk, in a mirror, or on your phone screen—as a daily reminder that you never face anything alone.

3. **Trade Fear for Faith.**
   When anxiety rises, pause and pray, "Lord, You are my strength." Replace every fearful thought with a promise from Scripture.

4. **Encourage Someone Struggling.**
   Gideon needed reassurance, and so do others. Find someone who feels weak or unsure and remind them of God's patience and power.

5. **Build Your Altar of Peace.**
   Set aside a few minutes this week to pray and thank God for His presence in your life. Like Gideon, name your moment of faith, acknowledge that *"The Lord is Peace."*

# For Discussion

1.  What fears most often hold you back from trusting or obeying God?

    _____

    _____

    _____

2.  How does Gideon's story encourage you when you feel weak or uncertain?

    _____

    _____

    _____

3.  In what ways have you seen God's presence turn your weakness into strength?

    _____

    _____

    _____

4.  Why is it important to remember that God's patience with Gideon reflects His patience with us?

    _____

    _____

    _____

5.  What "altar of peace" could you build this week—something tangible to remind you of God's faithfulness and power in your life?

    _____

    _____

    _____

# Samuel: Hearing God's Call

### 1 Samuel 3:1–21

*"The Lord came, stood there, and called as before, 'Samuel, Samuel!' Samuel responded, 'Speak, for your servant is listening.'"*

(1 Samuel 3:10)

**Class Overview:** In the quiet of the night, a young boy named Samuel heard his name called—once, twice, and then a third time. At first, he thought it was Eli, the aging priest, but it was God speaking. In that moment, Samuel's life changed forever. His story reminds us that hearing God's call starts with a heart that listens. This lesson explores how God speaks to those willing to hear, how He prepares His servants through obedience, and how a single voice of faith can bring renewal to a generation that has drifted from Him.

**Class Objectives:** By the end of this class, you should be able to—

1. Describe the spiritual condition of Israel during the time of Eli and Samuel.
2. Understand how Samuel learned to recognize and respond to God's voice.
3. Identify key principles for listening to and obeying God's word today.
4. Recognize the relationship between a receptive heart and faithful service.
5. Commit to developing a habit of listening for God through Scripture and prayer.

## Introduction

THE STORY OF SAMUEL'S CALL is one of the most touching scenes in Scripture. It occurs in the quiet of the night, well before dawn, when a young boy serving in the tabernacle hears his name called by God.

At first, Samuel doesn't recognize the voice; he thinks Eli, the priest, is calling him. But as the story develops, the voice becomes unmistakable. The Lord Himself is speaking.

Samuel's calling reminds us that God often speaks in quiet moments, not through thunder or noise but through a still and personal word. The boy who once ran to Eli would now speak for God to an entire nation. His willingness to listen marked the beginning of a life of faithful service. Samuel's story teaches that spiritual maturity starts with a simple response: *"Speak, for your servant is listening."*

During a time when few people listened to or obeyed God's word, Samuel's attentive heart stood out. God's call was not just about hearing, it was about obeying. What started as a child's voice responding in the night grew into the steady leadership of a prophet who led Israel for many years. His life challenges us to make space for God's voice, listen when He speaks, and respond with faith.

## *Historical Background*

The events of 1 Samuel 3 take place late in the period of the judges, a time marked by spiritual decline and confusion in Israel. The book begins with the words, *"In those days the word of the Lord was rare and prophetic visions were not widespread"* (1 Samuel 3:1). The people had largely turned away from God, and even the priesthood was corrupt. Eli, the high priest, was old and tired. His sons, Hophni and Phinehas, were priests in title only, lacking true conviction. They used their position for personal gain and dishonored the sanctuary (1 Samuel 2:12–17).

Amid this moral decline, God started a new work. Hannah, a humble and prayerful woman, had dedicated her son Samuel to the Lord's service at Shiloh. Samuel grew up serving under Eli, likely helping in the tabernacle—opening its doors, tending lamps, and doing small tasks. Though young, his heart was tender toward God. The spiritual silence that had marked Israel's condition was about to be broken through this child.

The tabernacle at Shiloh remained the main place of worship, housing the ark of the covenant. However, Israel's spiritual condition was dim, much like the lamp of God that "had not yet gone out" (3:3). This small detail reflects both the time of night and the state of the nation—the light of God's word was faint but still burning. In this setting, God spoke to Samuel for the first time. His call marked a turning point in Israel's history. Through Samuel, God would restore His word, judge corruption, and prepare the way for David's kingship.

Even in dark times, God is never silent. He stirs hearts that are willing to listen. The message that began with a young servant in the temple serves as a reminder to all of Israel that God still speaks and continues to call those who are ready to listen.

## God Speaks in the Silence

The story of Samuel's call begins with a vivid description of the times: *"In those days the word of the Lord was rare and prophetic visions were not widespread"* (1 Samuel 3:1). That single sentence captures the spiritual drought of Israel. God had not stopped speaking; His people had stopped listening. The priests were corrupt, the people were complacent, and reverence for God's word had faded. Yet even in that silence, God was preparing to speak again.

Samuel was still a boy, serving under Eli in the tabernacle at Shiloh. He was not yet a prophet or leader—just a servant performing ordinary duties. But the Lord saw something in Samuel that He did not see in many others: a heart willing to listen. When the text says, *"Samuel did not yet know the Lord; the word of the Lord had not yet been revealed to him"* (v. 7), it means he had not yet experienced personal revelation. He was faithful in service, but his relationship with God was about to deepen.

It was during the night, while the lamp of God was still burning, that the Lord called. The setting is both literal and symbolic. Darkness covered the tabernacle, but the light had not gone out. The silence was about to be broken. God called Samuel by name, "Samuel! Samuel!" but the boy, unfamiliar with the voice, ran to Eli. This happened three times. Samuel was eager to respond, but he mistook the source. Finally, the aged priest realized what was happening and instructed him, *"Go and lie down. If He calls you, say, 'Speak, Lord, for your servant is listening'"* (v. 9).

Those words reflect a heart ready to hear God. It's simple, humble, and willing. Samuel didn't yet know what God would say, but he was prepared to listen. That is the first step of true discipleship: making ourselves available before knowing the assignment. Many want God to speak, but few are quiet enough to listen. Samuel teaches that God's voice is best heard in stillness and obedience.

There's a clear contrast between Samuel and Eli's sons. Hophni and Phinehas were priests who ignored God's voice; Samuel was a child who listened. The difference wasn't in age or education, it was in the heart. God bypassed corrupt leadership to speak to a faithful servant. That same principle still applies. God speaks to the humble, not the proud; to those who are open, not indifferent.

When the Lord came and "stood there" (v. 10), calling Samuel by name again, it marked the end of silence. God's word was returning to Israel. The voice that had been quiet for years was now shaping the future through a willing boy. Samuel's simple response, *"Speak, for your servant is listening"* became the defining attitude of his life.

God still speaks in silence today. We live in a world full of noise, distraction, and confusion, yet God's voice remains the same. It still comes through His Word, His Spirit, and quiet moments of conviction. The question is not if God is speaking, but if we're listening. Like Samuel, we must make space for silence, humility, and readiness to hear. Spiritual renewal always starts when God's people say, "Speak, Lord, Your servant is listening."

## God Calls Those Who Are Willing to Listen

When God spoke to Samuel, He didn't choose a seasoned prophet or an influential leader. He chose a boy willing to listen. The difference between Samuel and the rest of Israel wasn't knowledge; it was posture. Eli's sons had hardened hearts and deafened ears. They treated holy things as common and ignored God's commands. In contrast, Samuel's heart was soft toward the Lord. Even before he recognized the voice, he responded to it.

The key to understanding this part of the story is Samuel's availability. Every time he heard his name, he ran to Eli and said, *"Here I am."* Those words, spoken three times before Samuel even knew it was God, show a spirit of readiness. When Eli finally realized what was happening and instructed Samuel to answer, *"Speak, Lord, for your servant is listening,"* Samuel obeyed. That simple response captures the essence of faithful service. God speaks to those who are ready to hear and respond without conditions.

When God called Samuel's name, He was doing more than awakening a child from sleep; He was awakening a nation from silence. Israel's leaders had failed to hear, but God found a heart that would. The Lord often begins His greatest works through those who seem least qualified but most willing. It was true of Moses, Gideon, Mary, and the apostles, and it is true here. God is not looking for perfection; He is looking for attentiveness.

Samuel's willingness to listen positioned him to become a voice for God. The message he received that night was not an easy one. It was a word of judgment against Eli's household. Yet Samuel listened carefully and delivered it faithfully. When morning came, he was afraid to share it, but when Eli pressed him, Samuel told him everything. His obedience, though difficult, confirmed his calling. Hearing God's voice means being ready to obey even when the message is hard.

This part of Samuel's story teaches an important truth for every believer: God reveals His will to those who are ready to do it. He doesn't speak to satisfy curiosity or pride. He speaks to guide obedience. Many people want to hear from God but on their own terms, hoping for affirmation rather than instruction. Samuel's example shows that a servant's heart says, "Speak, Lord," not "Explain, Lord." God calls those who are willing to respond without debate.

Notice, too, that Samuel's first act of obedience was rooted in humility. He didn't rush to proclaim that God had spoken to him. Instead, he waited until Eli asked. His restraint demonstrated maturity beyond his years. Even as God's chosen messenger, Samuel remained a servant. That humility would define his entire ministry. From this first encounter to his final days as Israel's prophet, he continued to listen before he led.

God still calls people with hearts like Samuel's. He speaks through His Word to those who are quiet enough to hear and obedient enough to act. His voice may not come audibly in the night, but it speaks clearly through Scripture, conviction, and the guidance of His Spirit. The real question isn't whether we can hear Him, it's whether we're willing to listen and obey. Samuel's story challenges us to keep our hearts tender and our ears open, ready to say each day, "Speak, Lord, Your servant is listening."

## God's Word Shapes His Servants

When Samuel finally heard God's message, it was not the comforting word he might have expected. The Lord revealed that judgment was coming on Eli's household because of his sons' corruption and Eli's failure to restrain them (1 Samuel 3:11–14). For a young boy serving under Eli's care, that must have been a heavy burden to bear. God's first revelation to Samuel was not about glory or greatness; it was about obedience to a difficult truth. This shows that God's word not only calls us into service but also shapes our hearts for it.

Samuel's reaction shows his humility. Verse 15 states, *"Samuel lay down until the morning; then he opened the doors of the Lord's house."* He continued with his regular tasks even after hearing such important news. There was no boastful tone, no rush to share what God had said. Instead, he quietly waited. When Eli called him and asked what the Lord had spoken, Samuel hesitated, unsure whether to tell him. But when asked again, he faithfully relayed the entire message, nothing more and nothing less. That moment was the true test of his calling. God's messenger must speak truth even when it's uncomfortable.

From that day on, Samuel's life became a model of faithfulness to God's word. The text states, *"Samuel grew, and the Lord was with him, and He fulfilled everything Samuel prophesied"* (1 Samuel 3:19). This indicates that God confirmed Samuel's words with His own authority. The young boy who once said, "Speak, Lord," became a prophet whose voice carried the weight of heaven. Everyone from Dan to Beersheba recognized that God had made him His spokesman.

Spiritual maturity depends on how responsive you are to God's word, not on age or experience. Every time Samuel listened and obeyed, his understanding grew. God's voice shaped his heart, and obedience built his faith. By the time he anointed Israel's first king, Samuel had spent years learning how to listen, speak, and act according to God's commands.

For us, the process remains the same. God shapes His servants through His word. The more we listen, the more we change. His word exposes sin, corrects our motives, and guides our steps. It teaches patience, endurance, and trust. As Hebrews 4:12 states, *"The word of God is living and effective and sharper than any double-edged sword."* It pierces our hearts so that our lives align with His will.

Samuel's story also teaches us that listening to God often comes with responsibility. Hearing His word means sharing it with others, even when the message is unpopular or hard to hear. Faithful servants don't change or tone down what God says, they deliver it with humility and love. Samuel's courage to speak truth to Eli opened the way for his role as a prophet who would later confront kings.

In every generation, God raises up people like Samuel: men and women who hear His word and let it shape their lives. Today, the church doesn't need louder voices; it requires listening hearts. Samuel's first response, "Speak, for your servant is listening," should remain our daily prayer. When we allow God's word to dwell in us richly, He transforms us into servants who can speak, lead, and live for His glory.

## Lesson Summary and Reflection

Samuel's call shows how God works in every generation. During a time when His word was rare and visions were few, God broke the silence through a boy who was willing to listen. Samuel's life reminds us that hearing God's voice starts with a heart that is attentive, humble, and obedient.

Samuel's experience teaches three key lessons. First, *God speaks in the silence*. When the nation was spiritually deaf, God called in the quiet of the night. His voice came not to the powerful or the proud but to one who was ready to hear. God's silence is never absence; it is often preparation. He still speaks through His Word and Spirit today, but we must slow down enough to listen.

Second, *God calls those who are willing to listen.* Samuel's readiness, his repeated "Here I am," demonstrates a servant's attitude. Before knowing the message, he made himself available. True faith says "yes" before understanding the full picture. That same willingness opens the door for God to work in us and through us. When He speaks, He expects obedience, not negotiation.

Third, *God's word shapes His servants.* The first message Samuel heard was one of judgment: a difficult message, not an easy one. Still, he listened attentively and delivered it faithfully. From that day on, God's presence and word influenced every part of Samuel's ministry. He learned that God's voice isn't given for curiosity but for obedience. The servant who listens must also act.

Samuel's story reminds us that spiritual maturity is not about age or position; it's about having a responsive heart. God is still calling His people to listen. The question is not whether He is speaking, but whether we are attentive. The same God who spoke to Samuel in the night now speaks through His written Word. He calls us to read, reflect, and respond with the same prayer Samuel spoke long ago: "Speak, Lord, for your servant is listening."

### Key Truths

- God still speaks in times of silence and spiritual darkness.
- A listening heart is more valuable to God than talent or position.
- True obedience begins with availability: "Here I am."
- God's word transforms those who receive and obey it.
- Hearing God's call carries the responsibility to speak and live His truth.

# Conclusion

We need to become better listeners. We live in a noisy world that values talking more than hearing and reaction over reflection. But God still speaks in silence, through His Word and providence. Those who pause to listen will hear His guidance, His correction, and His encouragement.

Samuel's response is the prayer every Christian should repeat: "Speak, Lord, for your servant is listening." That prayer transforms everything. It quiets fear, enhances discernment, and draws us into deeper fellowship with God. When our hearts are tuned to His voice, our lives will carry His message. The God who spoke to Samuel in the night still calls His people today: those who will listen and obey.

# Memory Verse and Weekly Challenge

*The Lord came, stood there, and called as before, "Samuel, Samuel!"*
*Samuel responded, "Speak, for your servant is listening."*
**1 Samuel 3:10 (CSB)**

**Weekly Challenge**

1. **Create Space for Silence.**
   Set aside ten minutes each day to read a short passage of Scripture and sit quietly before God. Ask Him to speak through His Word and give you wisdom for the day.

2. **Pray Samuel's Prayer.**
   Begin each morning with the words, *"Speak, Lord, for your servant is listening."* Keep your heart open to opportunities where God may be calling you to act or speak.

3. **Listen Before You Speak.**
   In conversations this week, practice patience and attentiveness. Listening to others often prepares us to hear God more clearly.

4. **Obey Promptly.**
   When you sense a nudge to serve, encourage, or forgive, don't delay. Samuel's story reminds us that obedience is the proper response to God's call.

5. **Encourage Another Listener.**
   Share Samuel's story with someone who feels distant from God. Remind them that God still speaks and that He often begins with hearts that are willing to hear.

# For Discussion

1. What distractions or "noise" most often keep you from hearing God's voice?

   _____

   _____

   _____

2. How does Samuel's readiness to answer, *"Here I am,"* challenge your own attitude toward serving God?

   _____

   _____

   _____

3. Why do you think God chose to speak to Samuel instead of Eli or his sons?

   _____

   _____

   _____

4. What does this story teach us about how God's Word should shape our daily decisions?

   _____

   _____

   _____

5. What practical steps can you take this week to develop a more listening, responsive heart toward God?

   _____

   _____

   _____

# PART TWO

# Prepared by Providence

*Now we will focus on how God shapes His people through His providence. Long before a task is assigned, God is already preparing hearts, circumstances, and opportunities for His purposes. This month's lessons demonstrate that God's preparation often occurs quietly—whether in the pastures, in the palace, or during trials— but His hand is always at work.*

*Esther reminds us that divine appointments are never accidental: "Who knows, perhaps you have come to your royal position for such a time as this" (Esther 4:14). David teaches that the courage to face giants is built in seasons of obscurity and faithfulness. Nehemiah's burden to rebuild begins with prayer and conviction, while Barnabas exemplifies how encouragement prepares others for greater service. Through these lives, we see that God's providence is active—it involves His ongoing shaping of His people for the works He has prepared in advance (Ephesians 2:10).*

# Esther:
# For Such a Time as This

### Esther 4:10–17

*If you keep silent at this time, relief and deliverance will come to the Jewish*
*people from another place, but you and your father's family will be destroyed.*
*Who knows, perhaps you have come to your royal position*
*for such a time as this.*
### Esther 4:14

**Class Overview:** Esther's story is a clear example of God's providence
in Scripture. Although His name is never mentioned in the book, His
presence is seen in every detail—from Esther's rise to the throne to her
act of bravery before the king. When a decree threatened to annihilate
her people, she faced a crucial decision: stay silent and stay safe, or risk
everything to speak out. Mordecai's challenge still resonates today: *"Who*
*knows, perhaps you have come to your royal position for such a time as this."*
This lesson reminds us that God places His people where they are for a
reason, and courage often means trusting His unseen plan.

**Class Objectives:** By the end of this class, you should be able to—

1.  Explain the historical background of the Persian Empire and Esther's
    rise to prominence.
2.  Understand how God's providence works even when He seems
    silent.
3.  Identify the choice Esther faced and what gave her the courage to
    act.
4.  Recognize the connection between faith, timing, and obedience.
5.  Commit to trusting God's purpose and acting with courage in the
    place He has positioned you.

# Introduction

ESTHER'S STORY IS ONE OF QUIET FAITH AND COURAGEOUS OBEDIENCE. She lived during a time and in a place where God's name was not spoken and His presence seemed hidden, yet His hand guided every detail. When a decree threatened to destroy the Jews, Esther faced a crucial decision: stay silent in comfort or risk her life to speak up for her people. She was an unlikely hero, a young Jewish woman in exile who had become queen in a pagan empire. But when it mattered most, she realized that her position was no accident.

The call that came through Mordecai still speaks to us today: *"Who knows, perhaps you have come to your royal position for such a time as this."* Those words capture the core of Esther's story. God's providence placed her exactly where she needed to be, and the courage to act was rooted in the faith that He was still at work, even when unseen. In moments of fear and uncertainty, Esther shows us that faith isn't just believing God can act, it's choosing to act because we trust that He will.

## *Historical Background*

The story of Esther takes place during the reign of King Xerxes (Ahasuerus), who ruled the vast Persian Empire from 486 to 465 B.C. His empire extended from India to Ethiopia and included many conquered nations, among them the Jewish exiles who remained in Persia after the Babylonian captivity. Although some Jews returned to Jerusalem under Zerubbabel and Ezra, many, like Esther and Mordecai, chose to stay behind, building new lives in foreign lands.

Esther's story begins at the royal palace in Susa. When Queen Vashti refused to appear before Xerxes at a royal banquet, she was removed from her position, and the king started searching for a new queen. Among the young women brought to the palace was Hadassah, better known by her Persian name, Esther. She was raised by her cousin Mordecai, who advised her to hide her Jewish identity. Through God's providence, Esther gained favor in the king's eyes and was crowned queen.

Years later, Haman, a high-ranking official, rose to power and demanded that everyone bow before him. Mordecai refused, and Haman's pride turned into hatred. When he learned Mordecai was a Jew, he persuaded the king to issue a decree to exterminate all Jews across the empire. Since Persian law could not be revoked once sealed with the king's signet ring, the situation seemed hopeless.

When Mordecai learned of the decree, he sent word to Esther, urging her to go before the king and plead for her people. But there was a problem: anyone who entered the king's presence without being summoned risked death unless the king extended his golden scepter. Esther had not been called to see the king for thirty days, and she knew the danger was real. Her initial hesitation was natural, but Mordecai's message reminded her that her position was not a coincidence. It was providence.

God's name is never referenced in the book of Esther, yet His presence is clear. He arranged events so that Esther was in the right place at the right moment. The story reminds us that God's sovereignty isn't limited by human power or political systems. He can work through unseen means and ordinary people to fulfill His will. Esther's courage to act in faith reminds us that God's purposes always succeed, and that He often calls His people to be part of that purpose, even at great personal cost.

## God's Providence Places Us
## Where We Are Needed Most

When Mordecai sent word to Esther about Haman's decree, her initial reaction was fear. She reminded him that approaching the king without being summoned could cost her life. In human terms, her hesitation made sense. She had no guarantee that the king would listen, nor could she predict the outcome. However, Mordecai's reply shifted her focus from fear to faith: *"If you keep silent at this time, relief and deliverance will come to the Jewish people from another place... Who knows, perhaps you have come to your royal position for such a time as this"* (Esther 4:14).

Those words reveal the central theme of Esther's story: God's providence. Mordecai didn't mention God by name, but his trust in divine purpose is clear. He believed that God's plan would not fail, even if Esther remained silent. The salvation of God's people was certain, but Esther had the chance to be part of it. That truth changed everything. Her position was not accidental; it was purposeful. Every event leading up to that moment, her selection as queen, the favor she gained with the king, even her concealment of her identity, had been directed by an unseen hand.

Providence means that God is actively working behind the scenes, directing events toward His purposes even when we cannot see Him. Throughout Scripture, God works through ordinary people in ordinary places to accomplish extraordinary things. Joseph's rise in Egypt, Moses' survival in the Nile, and Ruth's meeting with Boaz all demonstrate that divine coincidence is no coincidence at all. Esther's life follows this same pattern. She didn't seek her throne; God placed her there.

Mordecai's words also present a personal challenge. They remind us that faith is active, not passive. Esther couldn't just hope things would improve; she had to act. God's providence doesn't justify inaction; it calls us to participate. When we see that God has placed us where we are "for such a time as this," we begin to view every situation, our workplace, our relationships, our neighborhood, and our influence as part of His plan.

For Esther, obedience involved risk. To act meant facing danger; to stay silent meant losing the chance to save her people. But faith required her to trust the unseen God. In that moment, she realized that courage grows when we believe more in divine purpose than in personal safety.

The same truth holds today. God still places His people at specific times and places to fulfill His purpose. You may not stand before a king, but you might be in front of someone who needs encouragement, truth, or compassion. God has a way of arranging our lives so that we are exactly where He wants us to be. Like Esther, we often don't realize the purpose until we face a choice that tests our faith.

Mordecai's challenge remains: *Who knows? Maybe you are where you are for such a time as this.* None of us are in our current situation by accident. The jobs we have, the people we influence, and the opportunities before us are all part of a greater plan. God's providence places His servants exactly where they are most needed. The question is whether we will recognize His hand and respond with faith.

## God's Purpose Requires Courage and Faith

When Esther understood how serious Mordecai's message was, she faced a pivotal moment in her life. The choice was simple: stay silent and protect herself, or speak out and risk death. Persia's law was strict: anyone who approached the king without an invitation could be executed unless he extended the golden scepter (Esther 4:11). Esther hadn't seen the king in thirty days. Walking into his throne room uninvited was extremely dangerous. Still, faith called for her to act.

After battling fear, Esther made her decision: *"Go and gather all the Jews in Susa and fast for me. Do not eat or drink for three days, night or day. My female servants and I will also fast in the same way. After that, I will go to the king even if it is against the law. If I perish, I perish"* (Esther 4:16). With those words, she shifted from hesitation to faith. She didn't know how God would act; she simply trusted that He would.

This is the moment where courage and faith meet. Courage isn't the absence of fear; it is acting despite fear. Esther wasn't naturally brave; she relied on God's strength. Her fasting shows she didn't act on her own initiative. She first turned to the Only One who could grant her favor. True courage is grounded in prayer and dependence, not pride.

When Esther decided to act, her faith did more than change her future; it changed her people's as well. Her choice became the pivotal moment in the entire story. Because of her bravery, Haman's plot was uncovered, the Jewish people were saved, and the day of sorrow turned into a day of celebration. But none of that would have happened if she had chosen comfort over conviction.

God often invites His people to similar moments of faith. We might not face royal courts or death sentences, but we encounter choices that call for courage: standing for truth in a hostile culture, defending the innocent, forgiving those who wrong us, or speaking about Christ when silence seems safer. Each moment tests whether we will trust God's unseen hand or give in to fear.

Faith does not remove risk; it redefines it. Esther's words, *"If I perish, I perish,"* demonstrate complete surrender. She was unsure of the outcome, but she trusted God's sovereignty. That kind of faith depends not on knowing what will happen but on knowing who is in control. Like Esther, we are called to act when obedience calls for courage.

This part of the story also reminds us that courage rarely develops in isolation. Esther surrounded herself with others who fasted and prayed with her. She faced the unknown through community and reliance on God. Likewise, the church today needs people of shared faith who uplift one another during times of trial.

Esther's bravery serves as an example for every disciple. Faith involves trusting God's plan enough to act, even if we don't see how things will turn out. Courage means moving forward in obedience, confident that if God has called us to it, He will be with us every step of the way. Esther's choice to stand before the king was a quiet act of bravery; but in God's plan, that bravery changed history.

## God's Providence Works Through Our Obedience

When Esther decided to approach the king, she placed her life entirely in God's hands. Nothing in her plan guaranteed success. She didn't have the power to change the law or the influence to control the outcome. But she had one thing that mattered most: faith in God's providence. Her obedience became the channel through which God's unseen hand brought deliverance.

When she entered the royal court, the moment of truth arrived quickly. The king saw her and extended the golden scepter. That simple gesture of favor was not merely luck; it was divine timing. God had prepared the king's heart long before Esther ever stepped in. From there, the events unfolded with perfect precision: two banquets, the sleepless night that led the king to read the royal records, the discovery of Mordecai's past loyalty, Haman's downfall, and the eventual deliverance of the Jewish people. Every turn in the story demonstrates God's providence working through one woman's faith.

The book of Esther never mentions God's name, but His presence fills every chapter. The coincidences are too perfect to be random. The story reminds us that God doesn't need to announce Himself to be working. His providence often moves quietly, through decisions, delays, conversations, and even difficulties. While Esther may have felt alone as she entered the king's court, heaven was orchestrating every detail.

This truth offers great encouragement for us today. The uncertainty of our world does not stop God's purposes. He works through simple obedience, the small, faithful steps we take each day. Our job is not to control results but to trust God with them. Esther couldn't see how God would turn Haman's scheme into her people's salvation, but her obedience allowed God's plan to unfold. In the same way, our willingness to act in faith gives God room to show His power.

Obedience also brings peace. After Esther risked everything, she realized that God's faithfulness was enough. The fear that once controlled her heart was replaced by calm resolve. She had done her part and left the outcomes in God's hands. This is the core of faith: trusting that God's plan will succeed even when we cannot see it. As Proverbs 16:9 says, *"A person's heart plans his way, but the Lord determines his steps."*

For every Christian, the lesson is simple but deep: God's providence works through our obedience, not without it. He could have freed Israel without Esther, but He chose to do it through her. Similarly, He calls us to act, speak, and serve in ways that match His purpose. Our choices matter, not because they change God's will, but because they show our trust in it.

Esther's story ends with celebration, not fear. The people who once faced destruction now rejoice in deliverance. The day of mourning has become the feast of Purim, a yearly reminder that God turns evil into good and that faith-filled obedience can change the course of history. None of this would have happened if Esther had remained silent. God's providence was always at work, but He used her obedience as the spark that ignited redemption.

The same is true for us. The same God who placed Esther in the palace has placed each of us where we are. His providence surrounds us, His Spirit empowers us, and His purposes unfold through our choices. We may not see the end from the beginning, but we can trust the One who does. When we step forward in faith, as Esther did, we become instruments of His hidden, unstoppable plan.

## Lesson Summary and Reflection

Esther's story is a masterpiece of God's unseen providence and human obedience. His presence is unmistakable. He was working behind every event, from Esther's rise to the throne to her courageous stand before the king. Her life teaches that faith is not simply believing God can act but trusting that He already is.

First, we understand that *God's providence places us where we are most needed.* Esther did not choose her role or her circumstances; God arranged them. Mordecai's words reminded her, and us, that no one's life is an accident. Every Christian is where they are "for such a time as this." God works through everyday settings, homes, workplaces, friendships, to fulfill eternal purposes.

Second, *God's purpose calls for courage and faith.* Esther faced real danger when she approached the king, but she chose to act anyway. Her words, *"If I perish, I perish,"* demonstrate a faith that values obedience above safety. Courage does not eliminate fear; it overcomes it through trust in God's sovereignty. Her fasting showed where her confidence rested, not in human power, but in divine strength.

Third, *God's providence works through our obedience.* When Esther stepped forward in faith, God's hidden plan unfolded perfectly. The king's heart softened, Haman's plot fell apart, and Israel was saved. Each part of the story shows that God uses faithful obedience to carry out His will. He didn't need Esther to act; but He chose to work through her. The same is true for us. Our choices matter because they show faith in His plan.

Even when God seems silent, He is never absent. His providence weaves through our lives in ways we may not notice until later. Like Esther, we are called to recognize His timing and trust His guidance. Faith means believing that where we are and what we face are part of something larger than ourselves. When we obey, we become partners in the unfolding of God's redemptive plan.

**Key Truths**

- God's providence is always at work, even when unseen.

- Our position and opportunities are part of God's larger purpose.

- Courageous faith means acting in obedience despite fear.

- God uses the obedience of His people to accomplish His will.

- No situation is beyond God's ability to redeem and use for good.

# Conclusion

Esther's life challenges us to live with both courage and conviction. She started afraid, uncertain, and hidden, but through faith, she became a vessel of deliverance for her people. The same God who placed her in the palace has placed each of us where we are. Whether our stage is small or large, His purpose stays the same: to shine His light through our obedience.

You might not see God's hand clearly in your circumstances, but you can trust that it's there. Like Esther, you are part of His story. When you face moments of decision, when faith and fear collide, remember her words: *"If I perish, I perish."* Faith isn't about predicting the outcome; it's about trusting the One who controls it. And when we act in faith, God moves in ways that change lives and show His glory.

# Memory Verse and Weekly Challenge

*If you keep silent at this time, relief and deliverance will come to the Jewish people from another place, but you and your father's family will be destroyed. Who knows, perhaps you have come to your royal position for such a time as this.*
**Esther 4:14 (CSB)**

God's purposes will always prevail, but He invites us to take part in them. Every Christian is placed in their circumstances by divine design. Courage comes when we recognize that our lives are not accidents; they are opportunities to serve God's purposes.

**Weekly Challenge**

1. **Reflect on Your Position.**
   Consider where God has placed you, your home, work, school, or community. Ask yourself, *"What purpose might God have for me here, at this time?"*

2. **Step Into a Risk of Faith.**
   Identify one area where fear or hesitation has kept you from doing what you know is right. Pray for courage and take that step this week.

3. **Fast and Pray.**
   Like Esther, set aside focused time to pray for wisdom, courage, and sensitivity to God's timing. Seek His strength before acting.

4. **Encourage Another Believer.**
   Mordecai's words strengthened Esther's faith. Be a "Mordecai" this week—encourage someone who needs to see that God has a purpose for their situation.

5. **Thank God for His Hidden Hand.**
   Spend time in gratitude for the unseen ways God has guided your life. Write down moments where His providence became clear after the fact.

# For Discussion

1. When has God worked in your life in ways that you only recognized later?

   _____

   _____

   _____

2. What fears most often hold you back from speaking or acting with courage?

   _____

   _____

   _____

3. How does Esther's example help you trust God's unseen hand in uncertain situations?

   _____

   _____

   _____

4. Who has been a "Mordecai" in your life, i.e., someone who encouraged you to live out your faith courageously?

   _____

   _____

   _____

5. What step of faith might God be calling you to take "for such a time as this"?

   _____

   _____

   _____

## LESSON 7

# David:
# Equipped in the Fields

### 1 Samuel 16:6–13; 17:32–37

*"But the Lord said to Samuel, 'Do not look at his appearance or his stature, because I have rejected him. Humans do not see what the Lord sees, for humans see what is visible, but the Lord sees the heart.'"*
### 1 Samuel 16:7

**Class Overview:** David's preparation for leadership didn't begin on a battlefield or in a palace; it began in the quiet fields of Bethlehem. While others saw only a shepherd boy, God saw a man after His own heart. The skills David developed, faithfulness, courage, humility, and trust, were all forged in obscurity. When the day came to face Goliath, David was ready because he had already learned to rely on God's strength, not his own. This lesson reminds us that God often equips His servants in hidden places long before He calls them into public service. What we learn in the field prepares us for what we face in the fight.

**Class Objectives:** By the end of this class, you should be able to—

1. Describe how God prepared David through his early experiences as a shepherd.
2. Understand how private faithfulness builds public readiness for God's work.
3. Recognize that spiritual preparation often happens in ordinary, unseen moments.
4. Explain how David's confidence in God shaped his victory over Goliath.
5. Commit to trusting that God is preparing you—even now—for greater service.

# Introduction

When God sent Samuel to Bethlehem to anoint Israel's next king, no one expected it to be David. He wasn't the oldest, strongest, or most experienced. In fact, he wasn't even invited to the ceremony. While Jesse's other sons stood before Samuel, David was out tending sheep. Yet that's where God found him, faithfully doing ordinary work with an extraordinary heart. The Lord told Samuel, *"Man does not see what the Lord sees, for man sees what is visible, but the Lord sees the heart"* (1 Samuel 16:7).

That moment set the course for David's life. Before he ever faced Goliath or wore a crown, David learned to walk with God in solitude. The fields became his classroom. There he learned to worship, to fight off predators, and to trust God with every challenge. Those unseen years prepared him for every public moment that would follow. David's story reminds us that God's greatest preparation often happens out of the spotlight and without applause. When we are faithful in the small things, God equips us for the greater things to come.

## *Historical Background*

By the time of 1 Samuel 16, Israel was disillusioned with King Saul. Although he had started with promise, Saul's pride and disobedience led to God's rejection of his kingship (1 Samuel 15:26). God told Samuel to anoint a new king from among Jesse's sons in Bethlehem. This secret anointing marked the start of David's divine preparation.

David was the youngest of eight brothers and worked as a shepherd: a humble, often-overlooked role in that culture. However, this was exactly where God shaped him. Shepherding required courage, patience, and care for the flock: qualities that reflected the kind of leader God desired for His people. By defending sheep from lions and bears, David learned to depend on God's strength. These experiences laid the foundation of his faith when he later faced Goliath.

The contrast between Saul and David is eye-opening. Saul appeared the part of a king: tall, strong, and commanding. David was small, young, and unimpressive by human standards. But God was teaching Israel a new rule of leadership: outward ability does not equal spiritual maturity. The Lord wanted a king who would trust Him, not himself.

When David faced Goliath in 1 Samuel 17, he was still unknown to the nation. Yet, the courage that rose in him that day was not new; it had been built over years of quiet trust. While others analyzed the giant's strength, David remembered God's faithfulness. He said, *"The Lord who rescued me from the paw of the lion and the paw of the bear will rescue me from the hand of this Philistine"* (17:37). David's private victories had prepared him for this public one.

No act of faithfulness is ever wasted. God uses every small act of obedience, each trial, and every unseen challenge to shape His servants. The quiet seasons serve as the testing grounds for His kingdom. Before David ever wielded a sword, he carried a staff, and through that staff, God prepared a shepherd to become a king.

## God Prepares His Servants in Ordinary Places

When Samuel arrived in Bethlehem to anoint the next king, Jesse presented seven of his sons. Each looked like a likely choice. But God rejected them all, saying, *"The Lord does not see as man sees; man looks on the outward appearance, but the Lord looks on the heart"* (1 Samuel 16:7). Only after Samuel asked if there were any others did Jesse mention David, "the youngest," who was out with the sheep. While no one else saw potential in David, God did. The field where David worked was not a place of neglect; it was a place of preparation.

The shepherd's field became David's training ground for leadership. It was there that he learned responsibility, faithfulness, and courage. Day after day, he cared for his father's flock, protecting them from predators and guiding them to food and water. Those seemingly routine tasks forged the very character traits God would later use in him as king. Long before David led a nation, he learned to lead sheep. Long before he faced giants, he faced lions and bears. In that quiet place of duty, David discovered what every servant of God must learn: nothing is wasted when it is done faithfully before the Lord.

God often works this way in our lives. He equips us in ordinary, unnoticed places. The fields might not seem important, but they are where faith is developed. Many of God's greatest servants, Joseph in prison, Moses in the desert, and Ruth in the harvest fields, were prepared for big things through humble beginnings. The same God who shaped David in obscurity still uses hidden seasons to strengthen His people today.

David's time in the fields also deepened his relationship with God. Alone with his sheep, he learned to pray, worship, and depend on the Lord's presence. Many of the Psalms that would later bless generations were born out of those solitary moments of reflection. The heart that wrote *"The Lord is my shepherd; I shall not want"* (Psalm 23:1) was shaped by years of knowing what it meant to be a shepherd himself.

We live in a culture that values visibility, but God values faithfulness. He cares more about who we are becoming than how quickly we catch the world's attention. David's early life demonstrates that true preparation requires time. The quiet years are not wasted; they are sacred. They build the foundation for the moments when God entrusts us with greater responsibility.

So when you find yourself in a season that feels small or unseen, remember David. God may be using this time to prepare you for a task you cannot yet imagine. Faithfulness in the field comes before fruitfulness in the fight. The same God who saw David among the sheep sees you where you are today, shaping your heart for the work He has ahead.

## God Uses Past Faithfulness to Build Future Confidence

When David stood before King Saul, volunteering to face Goliath, his words revealed the quiet strength of a man shaped by God's faithfulness. Saul saw only a boy, inexperienced and outmatched. But David remembered what God had already done: *"Your servant has been tending his father's sheep. Whenever a lion or a bear came and carried off a lamb from the flock, I went after it, struck it down, and rescued the lamb from its mouth*

*… The Lord who rescued me from the paw of the lion and the paw of the bear will rescue me from the hand of this Philistine."* (1 Samuel 17:34–37)

Those earlier battles weren't random; they were rehearsals for this moment. Each time David faced danger in the fields, he learned to depend on the Lord's strength instead of his own. By the time he stood before the giant, his confidence didn't rely on weapons or armor; it was based on a track record of divine faithfulness. Every private victory prepared him for a public one.

God often builds our confidence in the same way. He allows us to face smaller trials first, teaching us to trust Him in daily struggles so we'll be ready for bigger ones. Every answered prayer, every moment of rescue, every lesson learned in difficulty becomes proof of His reliability. When new challenges come up, we can look back and say, "The Lord who helped me before will help me again." That kind of faith isn't just theoretical,it's proven through experience.

Notice also how David spoke about the Lord's role in his past victories. He didn't boast about his courage or skill. He said, *"The Lord who rescued me."* David understood that the same God who delivered him from wild beasts would also deliver him from Goliath. His faith was rooted in God's unchanging nature, not in his own ability. That is what distinguishes godly confidence from pride. Pride says, "I can do this." Faith says, "God has done it before, He will do it again."

Courage grows from memory. Remembering how God has acted in the past fuels our confidence today. When we forget His faithfulness, fear takes over. But when we recall His power and presence, fear loses its grip. This is why Scripture often calls us to remember, to recount God's mighty acts. Forgetfulness leads to unbelief; remembrance leads to faith.

For Christians today, the message is clear: the fields where you stand now are shaping the faith you'll need later. The small acts of obedience and trust you practice today are preparing you for bigger challenges ahead. God wastes nothing. The victories you gain now: over temptation, doubt, or hardship, are laying the groundwork for future courage.

David's confidence was not blind optimism; it was the result of tested faith. The God who had helped him before would help him again. And that same God still trains His people in the same way. Every challenge we face becomes both a test and a testimony. What God shows us in past faithfulness becomes the confidence we need for future battles.

## God's Power Triumphs Through Dependent Faith

When David stepped onto the battlefield, the odds looked impossible. Goliath was over nine feet tall, armored, and armed with weapons no ordinary man could handle. Israel's soldiers trembled, and even King Saul, who should have led the charge, stood paralyzed by fear. But David saw the situation differently. While others judged their strength against Goliath's, David judged Goliath's strength against God's. His perspective changed everything.

David declared, *"You come against me with a sword, spear, and javelin, but I come against you in the name of the Lord of Armies, the God of the ranks of Israel—you have defied Him. Today, the Lord will hand you over to me ... and the whole world will know that Israel has a God. This whole assembly will know that it is not by sword or by spear that the Lord saves, for the battle is the Lord's"* (1 Samuel 17:45–47).

These words reveal the core of dependent faith. David understood that victory would not come from his sling or skill but through God's power. His confidence was not in what he held but in whom he trusted in his heart. The phrase "the battle is the Lord's" captures David's entire outlook on life and leadership. Every fight, every challenge, every hardship belonged to God first.

In defeating Goliath, David demonstrated more than courage; he demonstrated theology. He recognized that God's glory was at stake. Goliath had mocked the living God, and David's goal was not self-promotion but defending God's honor. True faith always seeks God's glory, not personal victory. The sling and stone were just tools; the real weapon was David's trust in God's power.

God still works today through dependent faith. He doesn't need great strength or impressive resources to accomplish His will, He takes joy in using those who trust Him completely. Paul expressed this truth when he wrote, *"God has chosen the weak things of the world to shame the strong"* (1 Corinthians 1:27). When we trust Him, even our smallest acts of faith can produce great results.

Relying on God can look foolish to the world. Saul offered David his armor, but David declined it. He understood that worldly strength cannot achieve spiritual victory. Faith often asks us to let go of what seems logical and trust in what is faithful. David's confidence did not come from strategy or size but from surrender.

Every Christian faces giants: obstacles that seem too big to overcome. But the same God who gave David strength gives us strength too. Our "giants" may be fear, temptation, doubt, or opposition, but the principle stays the same: *"The battle is the Lord's."* We do not fight alone. God's power works through our trust, and His strength is made perfect in our weakness.

Dependent faith always points beyond itself. When David's stone struck Goliath, the victory belonged not to a shepherd boy but to the God who had trained him in the field. When we trust God completely, His power does what our strength never could. The field, the sling, and the stone all become instruments in the hands of a faithful God.

## Lesson Summary and Reflection

David's early life demonstrates that God's preparation is never wasted. Long before he faced Goliath, he learned to stand before God. His heart for worship, his faith in God's power, and his courage in danger were all developed in the quiet fields of Bethlehem. While others saw an insignificant shepherd, God saw a future servant being molded for great things. The same pattern remains true: God trains His people privately before He uses them publicly.

First, *God prepares His servants in ordinary places*. David's years with the sheep were not a delay but a purpose. Faithfulness in small tasks builds character for greater responsibility. When God develops His people in quiet places, He is shaping hearts that can withstand pressure and remain humble in the face of success. The work done in obscurity is often the most sacred preparation for service.

Second, *God uses past faithfulness to build future confidence.* The courage David showed in the valley of Elah was born from his experiences in the fields. Every lion and bear he faced was training for Goliath. Remembering God's faithfulness in the past gave him strength for the present. The same is true for us when we remember how God has helped us before; our fear fades, and faith takes its place.

Third, *God's power prevails through dependent faith.* David's victory over Goliath wasn't about strength or skill but trust. He stepped forward in weakness, relying entirely on God's power. His declaration, *"The battle is the Lord's,"* demonstrates the heart of faith. God takes pleasure in working through those who depend on Him. His strength is most evident when we recognize our weakness and give Him the glory.

David's story reminds us that our current situations are preparation. The unseen seasons of our lives, the daily tasks, quiet prayers, and unnoticed acts of obedience, are where God shapes us most deeply. He is building trust, courage, and faith that will help us when our own "Goliaths" arise. What matters is not how visible our work is, but how faithful we are to the One who called us.

**Key Truths**

- God often trains His servants in hidden, ordinary places.
- Faithfulness in small things prepares us for larger challenges.
- Remembering God's past faithfulness builds confidence for the future.
- True victory comes through dependence on God's strength, not our own.
- The battles we face belong to the Lord—our task is to trust and obey.

# Conclusion

David's story is about trusting a faithful God. The courage that faced Goliath was built through quiet obedience. The heart that led Israel was shaped in solitude. God's way of preparing us is often slow and unseen, but it is always purposeful.

You might feel like you're in the "fields" right now, doing everyday work, waiting for something greater. But remember, God is using this season to prepare you for what's ahead. Every act of faithfulness matters. Every step of obedience gets you ready. The same God who trained David is training you. When the time comes, you'll be prepared—not because of your strength, but because of His.

# Memory Verse and Weekly Challenge

*Then David said, "The Lord who rescued me from the paw of the lion and the paw of the bear will rescue me from the hand of this Philistine." Saul said to David, "Go, and may the Lord be with you."*
**1 Samuel 17:37 (CSB)**

See David's heart of faith. His confidence didn't come from skill or experience but from remembering God's past deliverance. Every servant of God can draw strength from the same truth: the God who has been faithful before will be faithful again.

**Weekly Challenge**

1. **Reflect on Your "Field."**
   Identify the ordinary places where God may be shaping your heart right now. Ask Him to help you see value and purpose in what feels routine or unnoticed.

2. **Remember Past Victories.**
   Make a list of moments when God has helped, protected, or guided you. Thank Him for His faithfulness and use those memories to strengthen your confidence in current challenges.

3. **Face One "Goliath."**
   Think of one area in your life where fear or doubt stands tall. Pray over it daily this week, declaring, *"The battle is the Lord's."*

4. **Encourage a Fellow Servant.**
   Remind someone else who feels overlooked that God often prepares His greatest servants in hidden places.

5. **Worship in the Fields.**
   Take time this week to pray or sing privately, as David did. Praise turns ordinary moments into holy preparation.

# For Discussion

1. How has God used ordinary or hidden seasons in your life to prepare you for greater responsibility?

   _____

   _____

   _____

2. What past experiences remind you of God's faithfulness and help you face present challenges with confidence?

   _____

   _____

   _____

3. Why do you think God often allows long periods of preparation before giving His servants public work?

   _____

   _____

   _____

4. What does it mean in practical terms to say, *"The battle is the Lord's"*?

   _____

   _____

   _____

5. How can David's example encourage you to remain faithful and dependent on God when you feel unnoticed or unimportant?

   _____

   _____

   _____

# Nehemiah:
# A Heart to Build

### Nehemiah 1:3–4; 2:17–18

*So I said to them, "You see the trouble we are in. Jerusalem lies in ruins and its gates have been burned. Come, let's rebuild Jerusalem's wall, so that we will no longer be a disgrace." I told them how the gracious hand of my God had been on me, and what the king had said to me. They said, "Let's start rebuilding," and their hands were strengthened to do this good work.*
### Nehemiah 2:17–18

**Class Overview:** Nehemiah's story is one of leadership rooted in compassion, prayer, and faith. When he heard that Jerusalem's walls were broken and its gates burned, his heart broke for his people. Though living comfortably as a royal cupbearer in Persia, Nehemiah couldn't ignore what was happening in God's city. His burden led to prayer, and his prayer led to action. This lesson reminds us that spiritual rebuilding always begins in the heart. God still calls His people to see the needs around them and to respond with vision, courage, and dependence on Him.

**Class Objectives:** By the end of this class, you should be able to—

1. Explain the historical setting of Nehemiah's burden for Jerusalem.
2. Understand how prayer shapes godly leadership and vision.
3. Identify the qualities that made Nehemiah an effective servant and builder.
4. Recognize that spiritual renewal begins with compassion and faith in God's power.
5. Commit to being a builder in God's kingdom—someone who strengthens, restores, and encourages others.

# Introduction

WHEN NEHEMIAH FIRST LEARNED ABOUT JERUSALEM'S CONDITION, he was far from home and living comfortably. As cupbearer to King Artaxerxes of Persia, he held a trusted and influential position in the royal court. But when news arrived that the walls of Jerusalem were broken and its gates destroyed, Nehemiah's heart was deeply affected. What others might have dismissed as distant history, he saw as a personal burden. He wept, fasted, and prayed for days, confessing the sins of his people and asking God to act.

Nehemiah's story begins not with building plans or blueprints, but with a broken heart. True leadership always starts that way, with compassion for the things that matter to God. Before God rebuilds a city, He rebuilds a person. Nehemiah's tears became the foundation of his mission. His prayer gave birth to vision, and his vision led to bold action. This lesson reminds us that spiritual restoration starts in the same way today, with people who see the brokenness around them and ask, "Lord, what would You have me do?"

## *Historical Background*

Nehemiah's story takes place around 445 B.C., nearly a century after the first Jewish exiles returned to Jerusalem under Zerubbabel (538 B.C.) and later under Ezra (458 B.C.). Although the temple had been rebuilt, the city walls remained in ruins, leaving Jerusalem vulnerable and defenseless against its enemies. The city's physical state reflected its spiritual condition: weak, discouraged, and exposed.

Currently, Nehemiah served King Artaxerxes I in the Persian capital of Susa (modern-day Iran). His role as cupbearer was one of great trust and responsibility, giving him access to the king's presence and ear. Despite his privileges, Nehemiah's heart remained committed to God's people. When his brother Hanani reported Jerusalem's shame, Nehemiah immediately felt its heaviness. The city that represented God's name and covenant was in ruins.

Nehemiah's response was admirable. Instead of rushing into action or blaming others, he turned to God in prayer. Chapter 1 records one of the most heartfelt prayers in Scripture, an honest confession of sin, a remembrance of God's promises, and a plea for mercy. His burden grew into a call as he prayed for favor with the king. Four months later, when the opportunity arose, Nehemiah courageously asked for permission to return to Jerusalem and rebuild its walls.

Artaxerxes granted his request, even providing letters of protection and timber for the project. Nehemiah recognized this as evidence of God's providence, saying, *"The gracious hand of my God was on me."* Upon arriving in Jerusalem, he quietly inspected the damage and then rallied the people to work. His vision united a discouraged nation, turning despair into determination.

The rebuilding of the walls under Nehemiah's leadership took only fifty-two days (Nehemiah 6:15), but its spiritual impact lasted much longer. Nehemiah's story shows what God can do through one person with a heart burdened for His glory. It also reminds us that the greatest work of rebuilding, whether in churches, families, or faith itself, always begins when someone decides to pray, trust, and act for God's cause.

## God Gives His Servants a Burden for What is Broken

Nehemiah's story begins with anguish. When he heard that the walls of Jerusalem were in ruins and its gates burned, his heart broke. *"When I heard these words, I sat down and wept. I mourned for a number of days, fasting and praying before the God of the heavens"* (Nehemiah 1:4). Though he lived far from Jerusalem, Nehemiah felt its pain as if it were his own. The disgrace of God's city and people pierced his heart. What others saw as an unfortunate report, he saw as a divine call.

This is where true service for God begins: with a burden. God often stirs His people not through comfort but through concern. Before He sends a servant to build, He first allows them to see what is broken. The burden we feel is often the seed of the mission God is planting in our hearts. Nehemiah's tears became the foundation of his leadership. His emotional response wasn't weakness; it was spiritual sensitivity.

Nehemiah's grief propelled him directly to prayer. He didn't hurriedly craft a plan or blame others. Instead, he fell to his knees and turned to God. His prayer in chapter 1 reveals a heart that recognizes both God's greatness and Israel's sin. He started by acknowledging who God is, *"the great and awe-inspiring God who keeps His gracious covenant with those who love Him"* (1:5). Then he confessed the nation's sins, including his own. He didn't point fingers; he humbled himself. Revival always starts that way, with repentance before action.

Nehemiah's burden also stemmed from love for God's name. He said, *"They are Your servants and Your people. Please, Lord, let Your ear be attentive to the prayer of Your servant"* (1:10–11). His concern wasn't for his reputation or personal comfort; it was for God's glory. The broken walls symbolized the shame of a people who once bore God's name with honor. Nehemiah longed to see that honor restored.

This principle remains true today. The first step in restoring anything, faith, families, churches, or communities, is to recognize the brokenness. God works through people who deeply care about His cause. It's easy to become numb to the brokenness around us: moral decline, spiritual apathy, division, and despair. But the story of Nehemiah prompts us to ask, *Do I see what God sees? Does my heart break for what breaks His?*

When God places a burden on our hearts, it's not to overwhelm us but to involve us. Like Nehemiah, we are meant to bring that burden to Him in prayer. The person who prays with passion becomes the person God uses with power. Before Nehemiah ever lifted a stone, he lifted his voice. His prayer became the starting point for renewal.

God still moves hearts in the same way. He grants His servants eyes to see beyond comfort and courage to act on needs. The burden may start with sorrow, but it always leads to action. What begins with tears often becomes a testimony of what God can rebuild through a willing heart.

## God Turns Prayer into Opportunity

For four months after hearing about Jerusalem's ruins, Nehemiah prayed. He didn't act immediately or speak rashly. He waited until God opened the right door. His prayer in chapter 1 ended with the request, *"Please grant Your servant success today and have compassion on him in the presence of this man"* (Nehemiah 1:11). "This man" was King Artaxerxes, the most powerful ruler on earth at the time. Nehemiah understood that only God could move the king's heart.

In chapter 2, that moment arrived unexpectedly. While Nehemiah was serving wine to the king, Artaxerxes noticed something unusual: Nehemiah's sadness. Persian law forbade expressing sorrow in the king's presence, but Nehemiah couldn't hide the burden he carried. The king asked, *"Why are you sad, when you aren't sick? This is nothing but sadness of heart."* Scripture says Nehemiah was "overwhelmed with fear" (2:2). Still, he spoke honestly about his ancestors' broken city.

In that moment, months of prayer became a divine opportunity. Nehemiah had no specific plan ready for that exact instant, but his time with God had prepared his heart. Before responding, he offered a brief, silent prayer, *"Then I prayed to the God of the heavens and answered the king"* (2:4). That short prayer demonstrates a heart trained by trust. It wasn't a lengthy plea but a quick act of dependence. God had opened the door; Nehemiah stepped through it.

His boldness was rewarded. The king not only allowed him to go but also granted letters of protection, timber for rebuilding, and authority to lead the work. Nehemiah immediately recognized that this favor was no coincidence: *"The king granted my requests, for the gracious hand of my God was on me"* (2:8). His success did not come from clever words or influence but from God's providence working through prayer.

This part of Nehemiah's story reminds us that prayer is not a replacement for action, it's preparation for it. When we pray, God aligns our hearts with His will and lays the groundwork before us. Nehemiah didn't manipulate the situation; he waited patiently until God set the right timing. Spiritual opportunities often come to those who remain faithful in prayer and watchful in spirit.

We can learn much from Nehemiah's spiritual life:

- He prayed first.
- He waited patiently.

- He acted when God opened the door.
- He gave God the credit afterward.

When faced with challenges, our first instinct is often to rush forward or try to take control. Nehemiah illustrates a better way: pause, pray, and trust God's timing. The same God who moved Nehemiah's heart also moved the king's heart. He guides the circumstances beyond our control.

God still transforms prayer into opportunities today. Sometimes, these opportunities appear suddenly, in unexpected conversations or decisions. At that moment, what we've cultivated through prayer becomes courage in action. The time Nehemiah spent on his knees prepared him to stand before the king. When we pray faithfully, we are never waiting in vain, God is working behind the scenes, preparing the way for His purpose.

## God Strengthens His People to Build

When Nehemiah arrived in Jerusalem, he didn't immediately announce his mission. Instead, he spent three nights quietly inspecting the walls, witnessing firsthand the damage that had broken his heart months earlier. He observed the ruins in silence before calling others to action. When the time was right, he gathered the leaders and said, *"You see the trouble we are in. Jerusalem lies in ruins and its gates have been burned. Come, let's rebuild Jerusalem's wall, so that we will no longer be a disgrace"* (Nehemiah 2:17).

Those words sparked renewal. The people who had become discouraged and hopeless were suddenly inspired. Nehemiah shared not only the need but also the evidence of God's favor: *"I told them how the gracious hand of my God had been on me, and what the king had said to me."* Their response was immediate: *"Let's start rebuilding,"* and Scripture says, *"their hands were strengthened to do this good work"* (2:18).

This is how God works: He strengthens hearts before He strengthens hands. The physical rebuilding of the wall started with spiritual renewal. God used Nehemiah's faith, humility, and example to inspire courage in others. Leadership that comes from prayer always builds confidence because it directs people back to God, not to human ability.

The task ahead was enormous, and opposition appeared quickly. Enemies like Sanballat and Tobiah mocked their efforts and tried to discourage the builders. But Nehemiah's response was simple and steady: *"The God of the heavens is the one who will grant us success. We, His servants, will start building"* (2:20). He didn't argue, panic, or retreat. He trusted that the same God who opened the door would finish the work.

Rebuilding God's work, whether walls, churches, families, or faith, always faces resistance. But the pattern stays the same: God calls, we obey, and He strengthens us. The people of Jerusalem didn't build alone. Each person took a section of the wall, working side by side, shoulder to shoulder. Every stone laid was a testament to unity and faith. The project's completion in just fifty-two days was nothing short of miraculous, a visible sign of God's favor and faithfulness.

Nehemiah's leadership shows that the strongest rebuilding efforts are driven by conviction, not convenience. He didn't seek credit for success; he gave glory to God. His repeated phrase, *"The gracious hand of my God was upon me,"* reminds us that God's strength makes everything worthwhile.

Today, our message is clear: God continues to strengthen His people to build. Whether you're restoring your faith, rebuilding a broken relationship, or working to renew your church, the process starts the same way, through prayer, trust, and determination to honor God's name. The same hand that guided Nehemiah's steps and empowered Jerusalem's workers is working in every believer who says, "Let's rise and build." When God's people come together under His purpose, no obstacle can defeat them. The walls are built, faith is renewed, and the world notices that "the gracious hand of God" remains on His followers.

## Lesson Summary and Reflection

The story of Nehemiah demonstrates what God can do through a single person with a passionate heart for His cause. Nehemiah wasn't a prophet or priest. He was an ordinary man serving in a pagan court, yet God used him to rebuild Jerusalem's walls and restore His people's hope. His story reminds us that revival starts when someone cares deeply enough to pray, trust, and act.

First, *God gives His servants a burden for what is broken.* Nehemiah's concern for Jerusalem wasn't casual, it was consuming. He saw beyond the physical ruins to the spiritual decay they represented. Before he ever lifted a stone, he fell to his knees. God still looks for people whose hearts ache for the things that dishonor His name. Every great work of renewal begins with compassion.

Second, *God transforms prayer into opportunity.* Nehemiah prayed faithfully for months before speaking to the king. When the moment arrived, his prayerful preparation built confidence in action. God opened doors no man could open and granted him favor before the king. Prayer doesn't just change circumstances; it changes us so we're ready when opportunity presents itself.

Third, *God empowers His people to build.* When Nehemiah arrived in Jerusalem, his faith motivated others to join the work. What seemed impossible became reality because the people trusted that "the gracious hand of God" was upon them. God's strength fueled their unity, courage, and perseverance. The same God who strengthened the builders in Nehemiah's time continues to strengthen His servants today to rebuild faith, families, and churches.

Nehemiah's story is about more than just walls. It's about restoration of faith, purpose, and commitment. It reminds us that God still calls His people to rebuild what is broken and to stand firm in the face of opposition. When our hearts align with His, He provides everything we need: vision, courage, opportunity, and strength.

### Key Truths

- God stirs His servants' hearts before He moves their hands.
- Every great work of faith begins in prayer.
- Divine opportunities often come to those who wait faithfully on God.

- God's favor empowers His people to persevere in the face of opposition.
- Spiritual rebuilding begins when God's people work together for His glory.

# Conclusion

Nehemiah's example encourages every Christian to be a builder. We live in a world full of broken walls: families needing healing, churches seeking renewal, souls craving hope. Like Nehemiah, we can't fix everything, but we can start right where we are. When we bring our burdens to God, He transforms them into purpose.

The same "gracious hand of God" that rested on Nehemiah also rests on everyone who trusts and obeys Him. Our role isn't to make things happen but to remain faithful while He works. God grants vision to those who pray, courage to those who obey, and strength to those who build. When His people come together with hearts dedicated to His purpose, even the most broken walls can be restored.

## Memory Verse and Weekly Challenge

**Nehemiah 2:18 (CSB)** — *"I told them how the gracious hand of my God had been on me, and what the king had said to me. They said, 'Let's start rebuilding,' and their hands were strengthened to do this good work."*

Nehemiah's leadership shows us that God's favor empowers His people to act, and His strength supports their work. Every act of renewal, whether in a city, a church, or a heart, begins when God's people trust His hand and rise up to build.

### Weekly Challenge

1. **Pray Over What's Broken.**
   Identify one area in your life, family, or congregation that needs rebuilding. Bring it to God in prayer daily this week, asking Him to guide your next step.

2. **Wait on God's Timing.**
   Like Nehemiah, practice patient faith. Instead of rushing to fix problems, seek God's wisdom through prayer before acting.

3. **Encourage a Builder.**

   Reach out to someone faithfully serving or leading a difficult work. Offer words of support and remind them that "the gracious hand of God" is upon them.

4. **Serve Where You Are.**

   Look for a way to help strengthen your local church—teach, volunteer, repair, or encourage. Building begins with simple acts of faithfulness.

5. **Give God the Glory.**

   At week's end, reflect on how God has worked in even small ways. Write down one example of His "gracious hand" in your life.

# For Discussion

1. What situations or needs around you stir your heart the way Jerusalem's ruins stirred Nehemiah's?

   _____

   _____

   _____

2. How can you make prayer your first response instead of your last resort when faced with a challenge?

   _____

   _____

   _____

3. In what ways have you seen God's "gracious hand" guiding opportunities in your life?

   _____

   _____

   _____

4. What opposition or discouragement threatens your commitment to "keep building"?

_____

_____

_____

5. How can you help strengthen the hands and hearts of others who are working to rebuild faith and hope today?

_____

_____

_____

# Daniel:
# Standing Firm in a Shifting World
### Daniel 6:1–23

*When Daniel learned that the document had been signed, he went into his house. The windows in its upstairs room opened toward Jerusalem, and three times a day he got down on his knees, prayed, and gave thanks to his God, just as he had done before."*
### Daniel 6:10

**Class Overview:** Daniel's faith was tested in one of the most hostile environments imaginable: the royal courts of Babylon and Persia. Yet through decades of cultural pressure, he remained faithful to God. When a law was passed forbidding prayer to anyone but the king, Daniel stood firm. He chose faith over fear, conviction over comfort, and trust over compromise. This lesson reminds us that a consistent walk with God builds courage to stand when it matters most.

**Class Objectives:**

By the end of this class, you should be able to:

1. Understand the political and spiritual background of Daniel 6.
2. Identify the habits that sustained Daniel's faith in a godless culture.
3. Explain why obedience to God sometimes requires civil disobedience.
4. Recognize that spiritual consistency is the key to moral courage.
5. Commit to living with integrity and faithfulness, even when it costs you.

## Introduction

DANIEL'S LIFE IS A STORY OF QUIET STRENGTH in a world that constantly changes. Taken from Jerusalem as a teen and exiled to Babylon, he spent the rest of his life working in pagan governments that often opposed his faith. Yet through every challenge, diet restrictions, fiery furnaces, and political schemes, Daniel stayed steady. His secret was simple but powerful: a disciplined, prayerful walk with God that didn't rely on circumstances.

By the time of Daniel 6, he was an elderly man serving under King Darius of Persia. His reputation for honesty and wisdom made him a target of jealousy among other officials. When they couldn't find any fault in his work, they attacked his faith. They persuaded the king to pass a law banning prayer to any god or man except Darius for thirty days. The penalty was death in the lions' den. Daniel knew the decree could not be reversed, but he also knew his duty to God could not be ignored.

When the law was signed, Daniel did exactly what he had always done. He went home, opened his windows toward Jerusalem, and prayed three times a day. That simple act of devotion became one of the greatest displays of faith in Scripture. Daniel's story teaches us that true strength comes from consistency. A lifetime of small, faithful choices prepares us to stand firm when the world demands compromise.

## Historical Background

The events of Daniel 6 occur after Babylon's fall, during the early years of the Medo-Persian Empire, around 539 B.C. King Darius (likely a regional leader under Cyrus the Great) reorganized the kingdom into 120 provinces, each governed by a satrap. Daniel was appointed as one of three administrators over them because of his outstanding character and ability. His integrity was so notable that the king planned to make him over the entire realm (6:3).

This promotion sparked jealousy among the other officials. Unable to find fault in his actions, they devised a plan to use his faith against him. They persuaded Darius to issue a royal decree that, for thirty days, anyone who prayed to any god or man except the king would be thrown into the lions' den. Since Persian law could not be repealed once enacted, the trap was set.

Daniel's response was steady. He didn't protest openly or hide privately. He continued his prayer routine , three times daily, facing Jerusalem and giving thanks to God "as he had done before." His faith wasn't reactionary; it was habitual. The same devotion that guided him peacefully also sustained him through persecution.

The story that follows, Daniel's arrest, his night in the lions' den, and his miraculous deliverance, reveals more than just courage. It demonstrates the power of consistent faith in an unpredictable world. Daniel's loyalty to God outlasted kings and empires. From Babylon to Persia, his influence remained because his character never wavered. God honored his faith, shut the mouths of lions, and used his life as a testimony that "He is the living God, enduring forever" (6:26).

## Faithfulness Begins in Daily Habits

When Daniel heard that the decree had been signed, he didn't panic, argue, or hide. Scripture says, *"He went into his house… and three times a day he got down on his knees, prayed, and gave thanks to his God, just as he had done before"* (Daniel 6:10). That phrase, *"just as he had done before,"* reveals the secret of his strength. Daniel's courage didn't begin in crisis; it was built through consistency.

From his youth in Babylon, Daniel developed a disciplined prayer life. Decades of walking with God shaped his beliefs and routines. He didn't choose to be faithful when the decree was signed; that commitment was made long before. His relationship with God was consistent, not based on circumstances. Whether in favor or danger, Daniel's rhythm of worship remained unchanged.

Faithfulness is often developed through routine. It's the unseen moments of prayer, devotion, and obedience that prepare us for visible tests of faith. Many people wait for a crisis to strengthen their relationship with God, but by then it's often too late. Spiritual habits built in private sustain courage in public.

Daniel's approach to prayer is also instructive. He prayed with humility, kneeling. He prayed with purpose, facing Jerusalem, recalling God's promises. And he prayed with gratitude, *"he gave thanks to his God,"* even as danger loomed. That posture of worship kept his heart anchored as the world around him shook.

For Christians today, Daniel's example reminds us to stay consistent. It's easy to remain faithful when it costs nothing, but true devotion lasts when obedience becomes difficult. The strength to stay firm during tough times comes from a life that walks closely with God in everyday moments.

Daily prayer, Scripture reading, worship, and gratitude are not small acts; they are the foundation. When the laws of the land conflicted with the law of God, Daniel didn't need to find his footing — he was already standing on solid ground.

The faith that silences the mouths of lions starts in quiet rooms of prayer. It's not formed overnight but over years of walking with God. Like Daniel, we must develop spiritual habits that will hold when the pressure increases. The consistency we establish today is the courage we will need tomorrow.

## Conviction Stands When Pressure Mounts

The officials who envied Daniel knew exactly where to find him: on his knees in prayer. They stormed into his home and caught him doing what he always did, honoring God. There was no hiding, no compromise, no delay. Daniel understood that obedience to God was more important than gaining men's approval. His faith wasn't rebellion for rebellion's sake; it was loyalty to a higher King.

When Daniel was brought before King Darius, the king immediately recognized the trap. He admired Daniel and worked all day trying to find a loophole to save him, but the law of the Medes and Persians could not be changed. Reluctantly, Darius ordered that Daniel be thrown into the lions' den. His final words were telling: *"May your God, whom you continually serve, rescue you!"* (Daniel 6:16). Even the pagan king had seen Daniel's consistent faith.

Daniel's courage under pressure didn't come suddenly; it came from deep conviction. Conviction is different from opinion. Opinions change with fear or convenience; conviction stays strong because it's based on truth. Daniel didn't know what God would do, but he knew what he had to do. He chose obedience regardless of what happened.

It's important to notice Daniel's calmness. There's no record of argument, complaint, or panic. His peace reflected trust. He had lived his entire life under foreign kings, yet his allegiance had never shifted. When governments changed and cultures clashed, Daniel's loyalty to God never wavered. The same man who had once refused the king's food in Babylon now refused to bow to Persian law. Faithfulness was his pattern, not his performance.

Conviction like Daniel's is desperately needed in every generation. Today, pressure comes in many forms, social, moral, cultural, and even legal. The temptation to blend in or stay silent can be strong. But Daniel's life reminds us that courage is not about fighting for power; it's about standing for truth. God honors those who honor Him, even when faithfulness brings suffering.

When Daniel chose to obey, he left the results up to God. He didn't know if deliverance would happen, but he trusted that God's will was best. That same trust supports believers today when faith is tested. Our role isn't to predict the outcome but to stay faithful to our calling. As Jesus said, *"Be faithful unto death, and I will give you the crown of life."*

In Daniel's story, conviction led to confrontation and to testimony. Even those who opposed him could not deny his integrity. When faith remains strong under pressure, the world notices. Daniel didn't just survive in Babylon; he thrived there. His unwavering trust pointed others toward the living God, even from the lions' den.

## God Honors Those Who Trust Him

When Daniel was lowered into the lions' den, the situation looked hopeless. The stone was rolled over the entrance, and the king's seal was placed on it. Humanly speaking, there was no way out. Nevertheless, Daniel's trust remained in God, not in rescue. He had depended on the Lord all his life, and that trust did not end in the darkness of the den.

That night, King Darius couldn't sleep. He refused food and entertainment, anxiously waiting for dawn. But Daniel, the condemned man, rested peacefully. He was surrounded by lions but protected by the power of God. Scripture says that the Lord "sent His angel and shut the lions' mouths" (Daniel 6:22). God not only protected Daniel, but He also proved his faith before the entire kingdom.

Early the next morning, the king hurried to the den and called out, *"Daniel, servant of the living God, has your God, whom you continually serve, been able to rescue you from the lions?"* (v. 20). From the depths of the pit came the calm reply, *"My God sent His angel and shut the lions' mouths... I was found innocent before Him."* (v. 22). That moment became one of the greatest displays of God's power in Scripture.

Daniel's deliverance was more than personal; it was a public testimony. Darius immediately issued a decree exalting the God of Daniel: *"For He is the living God, and He endures forever; His kingdom will never be destroyed, and His dominion has no end"* (v. 26). One man's faith transformed the heart of a nation's ruler and reminded the world that God still reigns.

This story teaches that God may not always remove us from the trial, but He will always be with us through it. Faith doesn't mean we will avoid the lions' den, it means we trust the One who rules over the lions. The same God who shut their mouths for Daniel still protects, strengthens, and upholds His people today.

Daniel's example also reminds us that faithfulness is never wasted. Decades of quiet devotion lead to one moment of public glory for God. Even when others plot against him, God turns every scheme into an opportunity for His name to be honored. When we trust Him fully, He writes stories that testify to His greatness.

Finally, Daniel's deliverance points us to an even greater truth: God saves His people through faith. The lions' den foreshadows Christ's victory over death. Like Daniel, Jesus was unjustly condemned, sealed in a tomb, and raised in power. Daniel's story is not just about survival; it's about resurrection hope. The same God who delivered Daniel from the pit delivers His people from sin and death through Christ.

When we trust Him like Daniel did, we gain the courage to face anything this world brings our way. The God who rules over kings and shuts lions' mouths is still active today. He honors those who honor Him. And when faith stays strong, His glory is revealed for everyone to see.

# Lesson Summary and Reflection

Daniel's story stands as one of the clearest portraits of unwavering faith in Scripture. He lived through exile, served under pagan kings, and faced laws designed to destroy his faith; yet he never wavered. His strength wasn't born from sudden courage; it was the fruit of a lifetime of walking with God. Daniel's life shows us how to remain faithful in a world that constantly shifts away from truth.

First, *faithfulness begins in daily habits*. Daniel didn't start praying when trouble came; he prayed because it was who he was. His consistency built resilience. The same habits that sustain us in peace will sustain us in trial. Prayer, gratitude, and obedience are not small disciplines; they are spiritual anchors that hold firm when life grows turbulent.

Second, *conviction stands when pressure mounts*. Daniel's refusal to compromise came from a settled heart. He knew God's truth and his responsibility to it. Courage is not about being fearless; it's about being faithful. Daniel didn't protest the law or seek revenge; he obeyed God and left the outcome in His hands. Conviction that endures is always rooted in trust, not pride.

Third, *God honors those who trust Him*. Daniel's deliverance from the lions wasn't just a miracle; it was a message. God used his faith to proclaim His power to an empire. Daniel's rescue revealed that the living God rules over kings, laws, and lions alike. Faith doesn't guarantee we'll avoid hardship, but it assures us of God's presence and power during it.

The story of Daniel calls us to stand firm in a shifting world. Our culture may change, but God does not. Like Daniel, we are called to live with integrity, pray with consistency, and trust with confidence. When our faith is tested, we can rest in the same truth Daniel knew, that "the battle is the Lord's," and His kingdom endures forever.

## Key Truths

- Spiritual strength is built through consistent daily faithfulness.
- Conviction is the courage to obey God when compromise seems easier.
- God's deliverance magnifies His glory to a watching world.

- Faithful obedience is the believer's greatest witness in a hostile culture.
- The God who rescued Daniel is still sovereign and faithful today.

# Conclusion

Daniel's story is about living faithfully in a foreign world. His courage was not loud or rebellious; it was quiet, steady, and unbreakable. The same God who honored Daniel's faith calls us to stand firm today. We may not face lions, but we face pressure to conform, stay silent, or compromise truth.

Faith that endures must be built before the test comes. Daniel's example invites us to develop habits of prayer, integrity, and gratitude that keep us close to God when everything else shifts. The world may change, but our calling remains the same: to serve the living God with unwavering faith. When we do, our lives, like Daniel's, declare that He alone is worthy and that His kingdom will never end.

## Memory Verse and Weekly Challenge

*When Daniel learned that the document had been signed, he went into his house. The windows in its upstairs room opened toward Jerusalem, and three times a day he got down on his knees, prayed, and gave thanks to his God, just as he had done before.*
**Daniel 6:10 (CSB)**

Daniel's strength was steady, thankful, and unshaken faith. It reminds us that consistency in devotion builds the courage to stand firm when the world around us shifts.

### Weekly Challenge

1. **Establish a Daily Habit of Prayer.**
   Choose specific times each day to pause and pray. Consistency, not length, matters most. Let this discipline anchor your faith like it did for Daniel.

2. **Stand Firm in Small Things.**
   This week, make one choice that honors God even if it's unpopular or inconvenient. Conviction grows stronger through obedience in the everyday moments.

3. **Trust God in the Unknown.**
   If you're facing uncertainty, write out one specific fear and pray, *"God, I trust You with this."* Leave the outcome in His hands, just as Daniel did.

4. **Encourage Someone Facing Pressure.**
   Reach out to a fellow believer who feels alone in their faith. Share Daniel's story and remind them that God still honors those who stand firm.

5. **Give Thanks in All Things.**
   Daniel gave thanks even under threat. End each day this week by listing three things you're thankful for—it's a habit that turns fear into faith.

# For Discussion

1. What daily habits in your life strengthen your faith and keep you grounded when challenges come?

   _____

   _____

   _____

2. How does Daniel's calm obedience challenge your view of courage and conviction?

   _____

   _____

   _____

3. In what ways are you tempted to compromise your faith under pressure?

   _____

   _____

   _____

4. How can you develop the kind of consistency Daniel showed in his walk with God?

_____

_____

_____

5. What does Daniel's story teach you about God's faithfulness and sovereignty in difficult seasons?

_____

_____

_____

# PART THREE

# Strengthened for the Mission

This final part of our study emphasizes how God empowers His people to fulfill the mission He has given them. Those He calls are continuously equipped through His Spirit, His Word, and His people. February's lessons highlight servants of God who relied not on their own strength but on the grace and power that come from Him alone.

Paul's conversion demonstrates that even a persecutor can become a preacher when transformed by grace. Timothy's story illustrates how faith and mentorship prepare the next generation for service. The church at Antioch shows us that congregations grow strongest when they serve and send. Paul's words to the Philippians remind us that God "is the one who works in you both to will and to work according to his good purpose" (Philippians 2:13). Each lesson affirms that strength for ministry comes not from talent or experience but from trusting the God who works through us to fulfill His mission.

# Mary:
# Faith to Surrender

## Luke 1

*"See, I am the Lord's servant," said Mary. "May it happen to me as you have said." Then the angel left her.*

(Acts 26:19)

**Class Overview:** Mary's story begins with a message that seemed impossible. A young woman from an ordinary village was chosen to bear the Son of God. Her world, her plans, and her reputation would all be turned upside down. Yet her response was simple and complete: *"May it happen to me as you have said."* This lesson teaches that genuine faith is not about understanding everything God is doing but about surrendering everything to His will. Like Mary, we learn that trust often means saying "yes" before we see how God's plan will unfold.

**Class Objectives:** By the end of this class, you should be able to—

1.  Understand the historical and personal setting of Mary's calling.
2.  Recognize how faith and surrender work together in obedience to God.
3.  Identify the fears Mary faced and how her trust overcame them.
4.  See how Mary's example teaches that God uses humble, willing hearts for His greatest purposes.
5.  Commit to surrendering your plans, timing, and will to the Lord's purpose in faith.

# Introduction

WHEN THE ANGEL GABRIEL APPEARED TO MARY, she was a young woman living in Nazareth, an ordinary town with little reputation. Her life seemed simple and predictable. She was engaged to Joseph, a carpenter, and preparing for marriage. Then everything changed. Gabriel greeted her with words that would change history: *"Rejoice, favored woman! The Lord is with you."*

Mary was deeply troubled, not because she doubted God, but because she didn't understand how such words could apply to her. She was humble and unassuming. Yet, God chose her for one of the most extraordinary roles in His plan: to bring His Son into the world. The message that followed seemed impossible: she would conceive and bear a son, even though she was a virgin. This son would be called Jesus, the Son of the Most High, and His kingdom would never end.

Mary's response reveals the true essence of faith. She asked only one honest question: *"How can this be?"* not out of disbelief but out of humility. When the angel explained that the Holy Spirit would bring about this miracle, Mary did not resist, bargain, or delay. She fully surrendered to God's will: *"I am the Lord's servant. May it happen to me as you have said."* That moment defined her faith, not because she understood everything, but because she trusted the One who did.

Mary's example shows that faith often starts where understanding stops. God doesn't always reveal His plans, but He always calls us to trust Him. Her story illustrates that surrendering to God's will isn't weakness; it's worship.

## *Historical Background*

The events of Luke 1 occur during the reign of Herod the Great, in the early years of the first century B.C. Israel was under Roman rule, and many Jews longed for salvation and the arrival of the Messiah. Mary lived in Nazareth, a small, overlooked village in Galilee, far from the centers of political and religious power. By all human standards, she was insignificant: young, poor, and from a humble town. Still, God's plan often begins in unexpected places and with unlikely people.

The angel Gabriel's visit to Mary occurred six months after his message to Zechariah about the birth of John the Baptist. Both miracles signaled the fulfillment of God's promises: the coming of the Messiah and the redemption of His people. Mary was probably a teenager engaged to Joseph, which in Jewish custom meant a legal betrothal. Breaking such a commitment required a formal divorce. The news that she would conceive before marriage posed significant personal risks: misunderstanding, social shame, and possibly even death under Jewish law.

Despite these dangers, Mary responded with faith. The angel assured her that this child would be conceived by the Holy Spirit, making Him holy, the Son of God. Gabriel's final words offered reassurance: *"Nothing will be impossible with God."* Those words anchored Mary's heart in faith. What seemed beyond reason was entirely possible with God's power.

Mary's story reflects the way God often acts. He chooses the humble over the proud, the willing over the strong. Her life demonstrates that surrender is not giving up, it is trusting in God's perfect plan. The child born through her would bring salvation to everyone, fulfilling the promise of Isaiah: *"The virgin will conceive, have a son, and name him Immanuel"* (Isaiah 7:14). Mary's straightforward yet deep faith reminds every Christian that when God calls, our best response is trust.

## God's Call Often Comes in Unexpected Ways

When the angel Gabriel appeared to Mary, his message completely changed her life. *"Rejoice, favored woman! The Lord is with you."* (Luke 1:28). Those words must have startled her. She was young, poor, and living in an obscure town. Nothing about her situation suggested importance or privilege. Yet heaven saw what earth overlooked. God chose Mary not because of her status, but because of her heart.

Scripture states that Mary was "deeply troubled" by Gabriel's greeting (v. 29). This reaction is understandable because God's call often comes suddenly, without warning or explanation. It disrupts normal life and invites us into something greater than ourselves. Mary wasn't seeking a mission; she was getting ready for marriage. But God had something eternal in mind.

The angel's words reveal the essence of divine calling: *"You have found favor with God."* That word "favor" doesn't mean ease: it means grace. God's favor doesn't promise comfort; it often brings challenge. Mary would soon face misunderstanding, suspicion, and fear. Yet in all of it, God's presence would be her strength: *"The Lord is with you."* That promise mattered more than any explanation.

Gabriel's announcement also teaches us something about God's timing. His plans rarely match our expectations. Mary was chosen at a moment that seemed impossible. She wasn't married, she had no power, and she couldn't understand how she would conceive. Yet God specializes in doing the impossible through those who trust Him.

Mary's humble question, *"How can this be, since I have not had sexual relations with a man?"* (v. 34), demonstrates both faith and honesty. She didn't doubt God's power; she only sought understanding of His method. Her question wasn't opposition: it was reverence. Gabriel's response directed her to the source of all divine work: *"The Holy Spirit will come upon you, and the power of the Most High will overshadow you."* (v. 35). What God commands, He enables.

Every Christian encounters moments like Mary's, when God's call goes against logic or convenience. It might come through a change in plans, a burden to serve, or a step of faith that feels beyond your strength. The question isn't whether we understand, but whether we trust. God's interruptions are invitations to grow in faith.

Divine calling always starts with grace, not merit. God chooses those who are willing, not necessarily the most qualified. When His purpose unfolds in unexpected ways, we can take comfort in the same promise Gabriel gave Mary: *"The Lord is with you."* His presence assures us that we are never alone in what He calls us to do.

# Faith Surrenders
# Before It Understands

After hearing Gabriel's explanation, Mary still couldn't see how everything would turn out. She didn't know how Joseph would react, how her family or community would respond, or what her future would look like. Still, her answer came quickly and without hesitation: *"See, I am the Lord's servant. May it happen to me as you have said."* (Luke 1:38).

That single sentence captures the core of faith: surrender before understanding. Mary didn't ask for details or guarantees. She didn't negotiate or delay. She simply committed herself to God's will. Her statement, *"I am the Lord's servant,"* shows total submission. She understood that her life was not her own and that obedience was more important than comfort or reputation.

True faith doesn't wait for a full explanation; it depends on God's character. Mary believed that if God called her, He would also support her. Her response reflects what every believer must learn: obedience comes before understanding. We don't need to see the entire plan when we know the One who holds it.

Mary's surrender was difficult. Her "yes" came at a price. She faced misunderstanding, rejection, and even danger. Under Jewish law, an unwed pregnancy could cause shame or death. Still, Mary's faith looked beyond fear to God's faithfulness. She trusted His power to fulfill His promises.

Gabriel's assurance, *"Nothing will be impossible with God"* (v. 37), was a declaration of divine truth. Every act of faith depends on that certainty. God's plans often challenge our understanding, requiring our trust to grow in step with His promise. Faith begins where human reason ends.

Mary's example challenges our modern desire for control. We often want to know every step before we obey, seeking certainty before committing. But God calls His people to trust Him enough to step forward in faith. Like Abraham leaving his homeland or Peter stepping out of the boat, Mary believed before she could see.

Her surrender also shows that faith is deeply personal. Gabriel brought a message for the whole world, the coming of the Messiah, but Mary's response was personal and immediate. She didn't try to understand everything about God's bigger plan; she focused on her part in it. That is what surrender looks like: saying "yes" to what God has put before us today, trusting Him with what comes next.

God isn't asking us to figure out His will; He's asking us to follow it. True surrender says, "Lord, I don't see how, but I trust You." And when we respond like Mary, we discover that obedience opens the door to great things.

## God Honors a Heart That Trusts Him Completely

After Mary's surrender, everything changed, but not in ways the world would call easy. She still had to tell Joseph. She still faced the whispers of neighbors. She still lived with uncertainty about what the future would bring. Yet through it all, she was sustained by faith in the God who had chosen her. The angel's words, *"The Lord is with you,"* proved true at every step.

When Mary visited Elizabeth, her faith overflowed in worship. Her song in Luke 1:46–55, often called *The Magnificat*, shows a heart that completely trusted God's plan. She praised Him not for making life easy but for keeping His promises. *"My soul magnifies the Lord, and my spirit rejoices in God my Savior."* Her joy didn't come from her circumstances but from her confidence in God's faithfulness.

Mary's trust allowed her to see herself as part of something much larger than her own story. She said, *"He has looked with favor on the humble condition of His servant."* She understood that God's work through her would bless many future generations. What started as a personal surrender became a worldwide blessing.

This is how God works: He honors those who trust Him humbly. Mary didn't seek recognition or greatness; she aimed to serve. Because she trusted completely, God acted powerfully. Her faith became the entrance through which the Savior entered the world.

Mary's life teaches us that trust doesn't remove hardship; it transforms it. God didn't spare her from pain. She saw her Son face rejection, suffering, and the cross. Yet she never lost faith in the God who called her. Her story shows that faith isn't about controlling outcomes but about trusting in God's goodness, no matter what happens.

For each of us, Mary's example provides both challenge and comfort. God still searches for hearts willing to say, *"I am the Lord's servant."* He rejoices in doing great things through those who trust Him fully. Surrender isn't weakness; it's confidence that God's way is best.

When we trust Him like Mary did, we find that obedience opens the door to joy, peace, and purpose that the world can't provide. God respects a surrendered heart. He takes everyday lives and fills them with extraordinary grace. The question is never whether God can do it; it's whether we are willing to trust Him.

## Lesson Summary and Reflection

Mary's story exemplifies clear trust and surrender in Scripture. When God interrupted her plans with a calling she couldn't fully understand, she responded with faith instead of fear. Her quiet words, *"I am the Lord's servant. May it happen to me as you have said,"* show what true belief looks like: humble submission to God's will, regardless of the cost.

First, *God's call often comes unexpectedly.* Mary wasn't seeking greatness or recognition. She was living faithfully when God chose her for a special task. The angel's announcement reminded her, and reminds us, that God enjoys using ordinary people to fulfill His eternal plans. His plans may surprise us, but His presence gives us confidence to follow.

Second, *faith yields before it fully understands.* Mary didn't need every detail before saying yes. She trusted that God's power would fulfill His promise. Genuine faith doesn't wait until everything makes sense; it believes that the God who calls is the God who enables. Surrender means letting go of control and resting in God's wisdom, even when the road ahead isn't clear.

Third, *God appreciates a heart that fully trusts Him.* Mary's obedience caused hardship, but it also resulted in blessing. Her willingness to believe opened the way for the Savior's arrival. Her life shows that trusting in God's plan brings joy that no circumstances can take away. When she praised God, her focus was on His mercy and power, not her own strength.

Mary's faith isn't just a story from long ago, it's a model for every Christian. God still calls His people to trust Him with the unknown. He still uses the humble and faithful to accomplish His greatest work. The lesson of Mary's life is simple: surrender is the highest form of faith. When we say, "Lord, may it be to me according to Your word," we place ourselves where God can do His best work.

### Key Truths

- God's call often comes to ordinary people in ordinary places.
- Faith says "yes" before it sees how God will work.
- Trusting God may bring difficulty, but it always brings purpose.
- Surrender is not weakness—it is confidence in God's goodness.
- God honors the humble and fills their lives with His grace.

# Conclusion

Mary's life serves as a timeless reminder that God's plans surpass our understanding. Her faith didn't eliminate uncertainty; instead, it turned it into worship. The same God who called Mary also calls us to trust Him with our future, fears, and lives.

When we surrender as she did, we find peace knowing that God is in control. We may not see how His promises will unfold, but we can trust in His faithfulness. Like Mary, our simple "yes" can become the beginning of something eternal. God still seeks hearts that will say, *"I am the Lord's servant."* That's where true faith starts, and where God's work continues.

# Memory Verse and Weekly Challenge

*"See, I am the Lord's servant," said Mary.*
*"May it happen to me as you have said."*
**Luke 1:38 (CSB)**

Mary's words are simple yet profound—an expression of total trust in God's wisdom and will. Her faith invites every believer to respond to God's call with the same humility and confidence.

**Weekly Challenge**

1. **Pray a Prayer of Surrender.**
   Each day this week, begin your prayer with Mary's words: *"I am the Lord's servant. May it happen to me as You will."* Ask God to help you accept His will with peace and trust.

2. **Release Control.**
   Identify one area where you are struggling to trust God—your plans, timing, or future. This week, intentionally release it to Him through prayer and obedience.

3. **Practice Grateful Obedience.**
   Like Mary, give thanks for what God is doing, even when you don't see the outcome yet. Gratitude strengthens faith.

4. **Encourage Humble Faith in Others.**
   Share Mary's story with someone who is anxious or uncertain. Remind them that God's favor is often found in simple faith and quiet obedience.

5. **Worship in Faith.**
   Read Luke 1:46–55 (Mary's song) aloud one day this week as an act of worship. Let her joy and trust inspire your own praise to God.

# For Discussion

1. How do you usually respond when God's plans interrupt your own?

   _____

   _____

   _____

2. What can Mary's humble acceptance of God's will teach you about surrender?

   _____

   _____

   _____

3. Why is it difficult to obey before you understand? What helps you take that step of faith?

   _____

   _____

   _____

4. In what ways have you seen God honor trust and obedience in your life or the lives of others?

   _____

   _____

   _____

5. What would it look like for you to say, *"I am the Lord's servant,"* in a specific area of your life this week?

   _____

   _____

   _____

# Peter:
# Strengthened After Failure

## Luke 22

*"Simon, Simon, look out. Satan has asked to sift you like wheat.
But I have prayed for you that your faith may not fail. And you,
when you have turned back, strengthen your brothers."*

### Luke 22:31–32

**Class Overview:** Peter's spiritual life is one of the most relatable in all of Scripture. Bold, passionate, and impulsive, he loved the Lord deeply, but he also stumbled deeply. The same man who declared, *"I will never deny You,"* would soon do so three times. Yet Jesus wasn't surprised. He had already prayed for Peter's faith to endure and had already planned his restoration. This lesson reminds us that failure does not disqualify us from serving God. In Christ, failure becomes the soil where humility, strength, and compassion grow.

**Class Objectives:** By the end of this class, you should be able to—

1. Understand Peter's denial and restoration in the context of grace.
2. Recognize that failure, when surrendered to God, becomes a tool for growth.
3. Explain how Jesus' prayer and forgiveness reveal the depth of His mercy.
4. See how restored believers are called to strengthen and encourage others.
5. Commit to living out your faith with renewed humility and confidence in God's grace.

# Introduction

FEW STORIES IN THE BIBLE CAPTURE BOTH THE PAIN OF FAILURE and the beauty of restoration like Peter's. He was one of Jesus' closest disciples, a leader among the twelve, and often the first to speak or act. He left everything to follow Christ and once boldly declared, *"Lord, I am ready to go with You both to prison and to death."* But just hours later, Peter would stand by a fire in the courtyard, denying that he even knew Jesus.

When the rooster crowed, Peter remembered the Lord's words and wept bitterly. That moment of shame could have ended his story, but Jesus had already provided for his restoration. Before the denial ever happened, Jesus told Peter that He had prayed for him, that his faith would not fail, and that, when he turned back, he would strengthen his brothers.

Peter's story reminds us that our failures don't surprise God. He sees them before they happen, and He offers grace to help us through them. What defines a believer isn't the absence of failure, but what happens afterward. Like Peter, we can be restored, renewed, and refocused for God's purpose.

## *Historical Background*

The events of Luke 22 occur the night before Jesus' crucifixion. After sharing the Passover meal with His disciples, Jesus warned Peter of an upcoming severe spiritual test: *"Satan has asked to sift you like wheat."* The imagery implies intense testing, a shaking meant to reveal weakness. Confident in his devotion, Peter insisted he would never deny Jesus. Yet, within hours, fear overtook him.

As Jesus was being tried before the high priest, Peter stood outside by the fire. Confronted three times about being one of Jesus's followers, he denied it each time. When the rooster crowed, Jesus turned and looked at Peter. That look pierced his heart. It wasn't condemnation, it was compassion. Peter fled, weeping in grief and guilt.

Yet failure was not the end. After the resurrection, Jesus personally sought out Peter. In John 21, by another fire on the shore of Galilee, the risen Lord restored him. Three times Jesus asked, *"Do you love Me?"* — just like Peter's three denials. Each time Peter answered yes, and each time Jesus responded with a command: *"Feed My sheep."* The same man who once cowered in fear would now lead the early church with faith. Peter's transformation from broken disciple to bold apostle shows the power of grace. God doesn't discard those who fail; He redeems them and uses their weakness to strengthen others.

## Failure Does Not Cancel God's Purpose

Peter's denial of Jesus was one of the most heartbreaking moments in the Gospels. Hours earlier, he had pledged his loyalty, saying, *"Lord, I am ready to go with You both to prison and to death."* (Luke 22:33). Yet, before the morning light, fear overtook him. Standing near a fire outside the high priest's house, he denied even knowing Jesus three times. When the rooster crowed, Scripture says, *"The Lord turned and looked at Peter."* (v. 61). That look broke him. He went out and wept bitterly.

It's hard to imagine the weight Peter bore in that moment: the guilt, shame, and disappointment. He had failed in the very area he believed he was strongest. Yet even as he fell, Jesus' earlier words offered hope: *"I have prayed for you that your faith may not fail."* Jesus didn't pray that Peter would avoid failure but that his faith would sustain him through it. That distinction is vital. Failure would not define him; grace would.

This truth extends into every Christian's life. Our failures, no matter how painful, do not surprise God. He knows our weaknesses before we stumble. Like Peter, we often make bold promises and then fall short. But Jesus' intercession guarantees that our story doesn't end there. His prayer for Peter: *"that your faith may not fail"* is the same kind of intercession He continues for His people today (Hebrews 7:25).

Peter's failure revealed two key truths: his weakness and Christ's strength. Left on his own, Peter's enthusiasm was not enough. But Jesus had already ensured his restoration. When Peter's faith wavered, Jesus' faithfulness remained steady. The Lord's plan for him had not changed. Jesus told him, *"When you have turned back, strengthen your brothers."* That meant Peter's biggest failure would become the foundation of his ministry.

God often uses failure to humble and prepare His servants for greater usefulness. Before his denial, Peter was confident in his own devotion. Afterward, he learned to rely entirely on grace. The man who once boasted would later write, *"All of you clothe yourselves with humility… for God resists the proud but gives grace to the humble."* (1 Peter 5:5). His pain had fostered compassion, and his weakness had become wisdom.

Your failure does not disqualify you from God's purpose; it refines you for it. The same Savior who looked at Peter with compassion now looks at us with mercy. He doesn't see us through the lens of our mistakes but through the power of His forgiveness. Like Peter, we can turn back, be restored, and help others find hope after their own failures.

Failure can shake your confidence, but it doesn't remove your calling. God's plan for your life is bigger than your worst moment. When you come back to Him in repentance, He not only forgives you—He empowers you to serve again.

## Grace Restores What Failure Breaks

After Peter's denial, we don't see him again until after the resurrection. The silence between those moments must have been heavy. He knew what he had done, and he knew Jesus knew it too. Yet when the women returned from the empty tomb with the news that Jesus had risen, they said something remarkable: *"Go, tell His disciples, and Peter."* (Mark 16:7). Those two words, "and Peter," were a message of grace. Jesus hadn't forgotten him. Even in failure, Peter was still included.

Later, in John 21, Jesus personally restores him. The setting was familiar, a fire by the Sea of Galilee, like the fire where Peter had denied Him. Jesus cooked breakfast for His disciples and then turned to Peter. Three times He asked, *"Do you love Me?"* once for each denial. Each time Peter answered yes, and each time Jesus replied, *"Feed My sheep."*

This wasn't about shaming Peter; it was about healing him. Jesus didn't lecture or remind him of his failure. He simply called him back to love and service. Grace doesn't ignore sin; it restores sinners. Jesus' questions let Peter reaffirm his devotion and understand that forgiveness also involves responsibility. His past didn't erase his future; it shaped it.

Peter's restoration shows how God's grace operates. It doesn't erase memories of failure but transforms them. The scars remain, serving as reminders of mercy. Jesus' threefold question gave Peter a fresh start, a chance to reaffirm what sin had taken away. The same voice that once called him from his fishing boat now called him again to follow, serve, and shepherd.

This is the power of grace: it meets us where we fall but doesn't leave us there. God restores what our sin destroys. He doesn't just put us back together; He remakes us for His purpose. Peter went from brokenness to boldness. The man who once denied Jesus out of fear stood just weeks later before thousands at Pentecost, preaching Christ with conviction. That transformation was not the result of human strength but divine restoration.

We need to understand this truth: God's grace surpasses our failures. His forgiveness isn't hesitant, it's deliberate. Jesus didn't wait for Peter to prove himself before restoring him; He reached out to him first. Grace always makes the first move.

If you've fallen, God isn't done with you. Your denial, regret, or mistake isn't the end of your story. Like Peter, you can return to Jesus and find not only forgiveness but also a new purpose. Grace doesn't erase the past; it crafts a new ending.

## God Uses the Restored to Strengthen Others

When Jesus told Peter, *"When you have turned back, strengthen your brothers"* (Luke 22:32), He revealed His plan for Peter's future. The failure that broke Peter would become the very thing God used to build others. Restoration always has a purpose. God doesn't just forgive to make us feel better; He forgives to make us useful again.

After the resurrection, Peter didn't hide in shame. Empowered by grace, he became a pillar of strength for the early church. On the day of Pentecost, it was Peter who stood before thousands and preached the first gospel sermon, declaring, *"God has made this Jesus, whom you crucified, both Lord and Messiah."* (Acts 2:36). The same man who once trembled before a servant girl now spoke boldly before the world. That's what grace can do.

Peter's failure humbled him, and his subsequent restoration softened him. He became a man of both courage and compassion. Later, in his letters, he encouraged believers suffering under persecution, urging them to *"stand firm in the true grace of God"* (1 Peter 5:12). He wrote as someone who experienced weakness and restoration firsthand. His message was powerful because it was born from experience.

This is how God works: He redeems our pain for His purpose. The lessons learned from failure become tools for ministry. People who have been forgiven deeply love with depth. Those who are broken become the best encouragers of others who are broken. Peter's story teaches us that the church needs people who remember what grace feels like.

Jesus didn't restore Peter solely for his benefit; He restored him to serve others. "Feed My sheep," He said three times. It meant, "Take care of those I love. Lead them, teach them, and remind them of My mercy." Peter's failure gave him the empathy and tenderness needed to shepherd others with grace.

Every Christian who has been restored shares the same calling. God doesn't waste your past. The shame you've conquered can become a testimony of hope for others. Your story of grace can uplift the weary, encourage the doubting, and lift up the fallen.

Our mistakes don't define our worth. In God's hands, restoration brings renewal, and renewal paves the way for service. The same man who fell hard was the same man God used powerfully. That's the story of grace, and it's still being written in every life that turns back to the Savior.

## Lesson Summary and Reflection

Peter's life serves as a strong reminder that failure is not the end. The disciple who denied Jesus later became one of the bravest spreaders of His message. His story shows that no matter how far we fall, God's grace can lift us even higher. What seemed like the end of Peter's ministry turned into the start of a new chapter, driven by humility, mercy, and love.

First, *failure does not alter God's purpose*. Peter's denial shocked him, but it didn't surprise Jesus. Long before Peter fell, the Lord had prayed for him and promised restoration. God's purpose is stronger than our weaknesses. Failure may shake our confidence, but it doesn't change God's plan for us. Through grace, broken people can be made useful again.

Second, *grace restores what failure breaks*. When Peter wept in guilt, Jesus came looking for him. On the shore of Galilee, by another fire, grace gave him a second chance. Jesus didn't erase the memory of Peter's sin; He redeemed it. That's how grace works. It doesn't excuse sin; it transforms the sinner. Forgiveness restores joy, renews a sense of calling, and rekindles purpose.

Third, *God uses the restored to empower others*. Jesus' command, *"When you have turned back, strengthen your brothers,"* became Peter's mission. The man who once fell became a shepherd of souls. His letters breathe compassion, patience, and courage because they came from a man who knew the weight of failure and the wonder of grace. God often turns our deepest wounds into our strongest testimonies.

Spiritual failure doesn't have to end in defeat. When we repent and return to Christ, He restores us, not only to forgiveness but also to service. The same grace that lifted Peter from shame can lift us from ours. God's mercy doesn't just cover our past; it equips us for our future.

### Key Truths

- Failure may bruise your faith, but it cannot destroy God's plan.
- Grace doesn't erase sin; it restores sinners to purpose.
- True strength comes from humility born out of forgiveness.
- God turns our brokenness into a ministry that helps others heal.
- Restoration is not the end of the story—it's the beginning of renewed service.

# Conclusion

Peter's life proves that grace rebuilds what sin destroys. Jesus didn't reject him for failing; He restored him to serve. The same Savior who showed compassion to Peter now looks at us with the same mercy today. He still says, *"Come, follow Me."*

Our failures can serve as our testimonies. When we turn back to Christ, He doesn't just forgive us, He gives us the privilege of helping others. Like Peter, we can go from guilt to grace, from shame to service. God's purpose for our lives isn't to leave us broken but to restore us and make us useful again.

So if you've fallen, take heart. Your failure isn't the end of your story; it's the beginning of something new. The Lord who restored Peter is ready to restore you as well, so you can go and strengthen your brothers and sisters in Christ.

# Memory Verse and Weekly Challenge

**Luke 22:32 (CSB)** — *"But I have prayed for you that your faith may not fail. And you, when you have turned back, strengthen your brothers."*

Jesus knew Peter would stumble, but He also understood that grace would restore him. Christ's intercession ensured Peter's future and demonstrated God's unchanging desire to redeem and transform every believer who turns back to Him.

**Weekly Challenge**

1. **Reflect on Grace.**
   Take time this week to think about a moment when you failed spiritually or personally. Thank God for His patience and mercy that brought you through it.

2. **Return Fully.**
   If there's an area of your life where you've drifted from obedience, return to Christ today. Confess it in prayer and trust His promise of forgiveness.

3. **Encourage a Fellow Believer.**
   Like Peter, use your own experiences of grace to strengthen someone who feels discouraged. Share how God restored and renewed your faith.

4. **Read John 21.**
   Reflect on Jesus' threefold restoration of Peter. As you read, imagine the Savior asking you the same question: *"Do you love Me?"*

5. **Serve Again.**

   Find one way to reengage in service this week. Whether it's helping someone in need, teaching, or praying for others—let restored faith move you to action.

# For Discussion

1. How does Peter's story change the way you view your own failures?

   _____

   _____

   _____

2. Why do you think Jesus allowed Peter to fail instead of preventing it?

   _____

   _____

   _____

3. What does it mean that Jesus prayed for Peter's faith not to fail? How does that truth encourage you?

   _____

   _____

   _____

4. How has God used your own past struggles to help or strengthen someone else?

   _____

   _____

   _____

5. What step of obedience or service might God be calling you to take as a restored follower of Christ?

   _____

   _____

   _____

# Paul:
# Bold for the Gospel

## Acts 20:22–24

*But I consider my life of no value to myself; my purpose is to finish my course and the ministry I received from the Lord Jesus, to testify to the gospel of God's grace.*
**Acts 20:24**

**Class Overview:** Paul's life was characterized by courage, endurance, and unshakable conviction. Once a persecutor of Christians, he became the gospel's greatest messenger. He endured beatings, imprisonments, and persecution, yet his passion never faltered. In Acts 20, Paul addressed the Ephesian elders, knowing he was heading toward danger in Jerusalem. Yet he proclaimed that his life had only one purpose: to complete the work Jesus had given him. This lesson calls on us to examine what drives our lives. Paul's example shows that courage doesn't come from strength but from surrender. When we value Christ above all else, fear loses its power. A bold faith is not reckless, it is rooted in grace and driven by mission.

**Class Objectives:** By the end of this class, you should be able to—

1. Understand the context of Paul's message to the Ephesian elders.
2. Identify the source of Paul's courage and confidence in the face of suffering.
3. Recognize that gospel boldness grows from deep conviction and eternal perspective.
4. Learn how grace and mission shaped Paul's purpose.
5. Commit to living courageously for Christ, regardless of cost or consequence.

# Introduction

Paul's journey of faith was anything but easy. From the moment of his conversion on the road to Damascus, he knew that following Jesus would bring suffering. Yet he never turned back. Whether before kings or in chains, his message remained the same: *"Jesus Christ is Lord."*

In Acts 20, Paul was traveling to Jerusalem, fully aware that hardships awaited him. The Holy Spirit had warned him that imprisonment and persecution were certain. Yet rather than retreat, he pressed on. To the elders of the church in Ephesus, he spoke with deep conviction: *"I am compelled by the Spirit ... not knowing what I will encounter there, except that in every town the Holy Spirit warns me that chains and afflictions are waiting for me."* (Acts 20:22–23).

Most people would have turned back. Paul kept going. His courage wasn't based on optimism, it was grounded in purpose. He said, *"I consider my life of no value to myself; my purpose is to finish my course and the ministry I received from the Lord Jesus."* For Paul, the mission outweighed the risk. He lived and breathed for one thing: to proclaim the gospel of God's grace. Boldness for Christ comes from conviction. When the love of Christ defines us, fear loses its grip. The more we understand God's grace, the more courageously we can share it.

## *Historical Background*

Acts 20 records Paul's farewell speech to the Ephesian elders during his third missionary journey. He was traveling from Corinth to Jerusalem with financial aid for the poor believers there (Romans 15:25–26). On his way, he stopped at Miletus and called for the elders of the church in Ephesus, a congregation he had served for three years.

Paul's message to them is filled with deep emotion and concern. He revisited his time among them, recalled the hardships he endured, and warned about false teachers who would come. But his focus was not on himself; it was on the gospel and the faithfulness it calls for.

Paul understood that suffering awaited him in Jerusalem, possibly even death. Still, his resolve was unwavering. The phrase *"I am compelled by the Spirit"* (v. 22) reflects his obedience to God's guidance, not his personal desire. For Paul, obedience was more valuable than safety. His confidence did not rest in his ability to persevere but in God's faithfulness, who called him.

Throughout his ministry, Paul endured significant trials: stoning, imprisonment, rejection, and betrayal. But rather than break him, these experiences strengthened his reliance on grace. The same grace that saved him on the road to Damascus supported him through every hardship. By the time he addressed the Ephesian elders, Paul had learned that courage isn't the absence of fear, it's the choice to obey God despite it.

## Courage Flows from Conviction

Paul's boldness wasn't reckless emotion; it was rooted in conviction. He understood why he lived and what mattered most. *"I am compelled by the Spirit,"* he said, *"not knowing what I will encounter there."* (Acts 20:22). That phrase reveals the source of his courage: obedience to God's will. Paul wasn't motivated by comfort or safety but by the certainty of his calling.

Conviction provides direction. Many people act based on preferences, doing what feels right in the moment. Paul lived with purpose. His conviction about the gospel gave him clarity, even when the future was uncertain. He knew hardship was coming, but he refused to let fear control his decisions. The Holy Spirit had repeatedly warned him that "chains and afflictions" awaited, yet Paul kept moving forward. He had already counted the cost, and his mind was made up.

This kind of courage doesn't come from personality; it comes from perspective. Paul understood that his life belonged to Christ. When he said, *"I consider my life of no value to myself,"* he wasn't being careless about life; he was being clear about priorities. To him, living for Christ was worth any suffering. He later wrote, *"I no longer live, but Christ lives in me."* (Galatians 2:20).

Conviction stems from a relationship. Paul's courage didn't come from self-confidence but from genuinely knowing the Savior. He had seen the risen Lord and experienced the transforming power of grace. That experience settled his allegiance in his heart forever. Once grace captures someone's heart, fear loses its grip.

For us, Paul's example is both inspiring and convicting. The world around us often values comfort, security, and approval. But courage for the gospel demands a conviction deeper than those things. It means obeying God even when it costs us friends, reputation, or safety. True conviction says, "My purpose is greater than my pain."

The courage to stay strong doesn't come from removing fear; it comes from focusing on something greater than fear. He wasn't fearless; he was faithful. The Holy Spirit urged him to move forward, and that was enough.

The same Spirit still empowers believers today. When we understand who we belong to and our purpose, courage naturally follows conviction. Like Paul, we can say, *"None of these things move me."* Our calling to spread the gospel surpasses any threat the world can present.

## Grace Gives Strength to Endure

Paul's courage was fueled by something deeper than determination; it was rooted in grace. He said his mission was *"to testify to the gospel of God's grace."* (Acts 20:24). Grace wasn't just his message; it was his motivation. Every trial he faced, every hardship he endured, became another opportunity to demonstrate what God's grace can do in a surrendered life.

From the start of his ministry, Paul understood that following Christ would involve suffering. Jesus had told him, *"I will show him how much he must suffer for My name."* (Acts 9:16). Still, Paul never complained or backed away. He saw grace not to avoid pain, but as strength to endure it. Grace didn't make his journey easier; it made him steadfast.

Throughout his letters, Paul described grace as the sustaining power of his ministry. When he faced weakness, he heard the Lord say, *"My grace is sufficient for you, for My power is perfected in weakness."* (2 Corinthians 12:9). That truth became his anchor. Grace didn't remove the burden; it gave him the strength to carry it.

Paul's endurance wasn't due to mere willpower; it was the result of faith. He trusted that whatever he faced was under God's control. Every beating, imprisonment, and rejection served as a reminder that God's strength was sufficient. That's why he could write from prison, *"I can do all things through Christ who strengthens me."* (Philippians 4:13)

Grace also brought joy to Paul during difficult times. In Acts 16, he sang hymns while in jail. In 2 Corinthians, he described his hardships as "light and momentary troubles" compared to eternal glory. His outlook was shaped not by pain but by promise. Grace helped him see beyond the immediate to the bigger purpose.

For us today, this truth remains: the same grace that saved us is the same grace that sustains us. We may not face persecution like Paul did, but we all encounter pressures that test our faith. The answer remains the same: depend on grace. When life feels overwhelming, when the cost of faith seems high, remember that the God who called you will also carry you.

Grace doesn't mean life will be easy. It means God will be enough. Paul endured because he never stopped relying on the One who met him on the Damascus road. Every challenge became an opportunity to show the sufficiency of Christ. If you want lasting courage, anchor your heart in grace. Let God's mercy be your motivation and His strength your support. Like Paul, you'll find that grace doesn't just save you; it keeps you standing when everything else gives way.

## The Mission Matters More Than the Cost

Paul's words in Acts 20:24 summarize his life: *"My purpose is to finish my course and the ministry I received from the Lord Jesus, to testify to the gospel of God's grace."* That sentence explains why he was fearless. His purpose was clear. His mission, to proclaim the good news, was worth more than comfort, safety, or even life itself.

Paul knew what awaited him in Jerusalem: imprisonment, persecution, and suffering. But he wasn't motivated by self-preservation; he was motivated by obedience. He had surrendered the right to control his own life the moment he met Christ. Everything after that moment was lived for one purpose: to complete the work God had assigned him.

This mindset shaped Paul's entire ministry. He viewed every situation as an opportunity to share the gospel. When imprisoned, he preached to the guards. When shipwrecked, he encouraged his shipmates. When faced with opposition, he reasoned with his accusers. Paul couldn't be stopped because his life wasn't focused on avoiding hardship; it was focused on spreading truth.

The secret to his courage was perspective. He saw suffering as temporary and reward as everlasting. He wrote later, *"I consider that the sufferings of this present time are not worth comparing with the glory that is going to be revealed to us."* (Romans 8:18). The mission gave purpose to every hardship. When your life's goal is eternal, no earthly cost feels too high.

Paul's determination challenges modern followers to consider what truly motivates us. Too often, we allow fear, convenience, or comfort to shape our obedience. But Paul reminds us that the gospel is worth everything we have. The Christian life isn't about saving ourselves; it's about giving fully for the sake of Christ.

Near the end of his life, Paul could say with confidence, *"I have fought the good fight, I have finished the race, I have kept the faith."* (2 Timothy 4:7). That statement wasn't pride, it was peace. He had done what God called him to do. His life, though full of suffering, was a story of victory because it was spent for something that lasted.

Paul's example shows us that true boldness isn't reckless, and sacrifice isn't a loss. When our goal is to glorify Christ, every act of obedience is a gain. The courage to endure comes from understanding that the cost of following Jesus is temporary, but the reward lasts forever. Like Paul, we must decide what matters most. When Christ and His gospel become our highest purpose, we'll find strength to keep going, no matter the cost.

# Lesson Summary and Reflection

Paul's life illustrates what it means to live with unwavering focus on the gospel. From the moment Jesus met him on the Damascus road, everything changed. His plans, priorities, and ambitions were replaced with a single passion, to complete the work God gave him. Even as suffering and death approached, Paul continued with joy because his purpose was clear, and his confidence was in Christ.

First, *courage comes from conviction*. Paul didn't act on impulse but with purpose. He was "compelled by the Spirit," not driven by fear. His bravery was rooted in clarity; he knew who he served and why. Conviction provides direction. When God's will is our foundation, we stop asking, "What will this cost me?" and begin asking, "What will glorify Christ?"

Second, *grace provides strength to persevere*. Paul faced numerous trials, beatings, imprisonments, and betrayals, but he never gave up because he depended on grace. The same grace that saved him also empowered him. He discovered that weakness was the very place where God's power proved to be the strongest. Grace didn't take away his suffering; it redeemed it. Through everything, Paul's life proclaimed, "Christ is enough."

Third, *the mission is more important than the cost*. Paul's eyes were fixed on the finish line. He understood that his calling was greater than his comfort. The gospel was worth any sacrifice. For him, to live was Christ and to die was gain. This perspective frees us from fear. When eternity shapes our priorities, we can serve boldly, love deeply, and endure faithfully.

Paul's example challenges us today to evaluate what motivates us. Do we prioritize ease or mission? Are our choices driven by comfort or conviction? The gospel calls us to join Paul in proclaiming that our lives have one ultimate purpose—to testify to the grace of God.

**Key Truths**

- Boldness for the gospel comes from deep conviction, not emotion.
- Grace is both the message we share and the strength we stand on.
- Obedience to God matters more than personal comfort or safety.
- Eternal purpose gives meaning to temporary pain.
- A faithful finish is the genuine measure of a life lived for Christ.

# Conclusion

Paul's life was filled with hardship, but it was never empty. Every step, every scar, every sacrifice pointed others to the Savior. His courage didn't come from self-confidence; it came from knowing his mission and trusting God's power.

The same call that compelled Paul still calls us today: to live boldly for the gospel of grace. The world needs to see us as people who value Christ more than comfort, who obey God regardless of the outcome, and who finish their race with faith and joy.

When we live with that kind of focus, fear loses its grip, and our lives become living testimonies of grace. Like Paul, may we say, *"My life is worth nothing to me unless I use it for the work assigned to me by the Lord Jesus."* That is the boldness that changes the world.

# Memory Verse and Weekly Challenge

**Acts 20:24 (CSB)** — *"But I consider my life of no value to myself; my purpose is to finish my course and the ministry I received from the Lord Jesus, to testify to the gospel of God's grace."*

Paul saw his life through the lens of mission, not self-preservation. For him, every breath was an opportunity to proclaim God's grace, regardless of cost.

**Weekly Challenge**

1. **Clarify Your Purpose.**
   Write out in one sentence what you believe God has called you to do in this season of life. Ask Him to renew your conviction to live that purpose daily.

2. **Pray for Courage.**
   Each day this week, pray specifically for boldness to speak or act for Christ—even when it's uncomfortable. Ask God to give you Paul's heart for obedience.

3. **Depend on Grace.**
   Reflect on how God's grace has strengthened you in past challenges. Thank Him for sustaining you and trust Him for the strength you'll need ahead.

4. **Take One Gospel Step.**
   Share your faith in a simple, genuine way this week: through a conversation, an invitation, or an act of service that points others to Jesus.

5. **Evaluate Your Priorities.**
   At week's end, ask: "What matters most to me, comfort or calling?" Pray for a heart that values the mission more than the cost.

# For Discussion

1. What truths or convictions give you courage to live boldly for Christ?

   _____

   _____

   _____

2. How does Paul's example challenge the way you handle fear, pressure, or hardship?

   _____

   _____

   _____

3. Where do you need to rely more on God's grace instead of your own strength?

   _____

   _____

   _____

4. What might it look like in your life to value the mission of Christ above personal comfort?

   _____

   _____

   _____

5. How can you help encourage boldness and endurance in others who are serving alongside you?

   _____

   _____

   _____

# Jesus:
# The Perfect Example
### Hebrews 12:1–3

*Keeping our eyes on Jesus, the pioneer and perfecter of our faith.*
*For the joy that lay before Him, He endured the cross, despising the shame,*
*and sat down at the right hand of the throne of God.*
### Hebrews 12:2

**Class Overview:** All the examples of faith in Scripture ultimately point to one: the Lord Jesus Christ. He is not only the model of faith but its source and completion. The writer of Hebrews calls believers to fix their eyes on Him, especially when life feels heavy or discouraging. Jesus' endurance through suffering and shame shows us how to remain faithful when we face our own trials.

This lesson reminds us that the Christian life is not about running perfectly but about running persistently, with eyes on the One who finished the race before us. Jesus' victory gives us strength to endure, courage to obey, and hope that our suffering is never wasted.

**Class Objectives:** By the end of this class, you should be able to—

1. Understand how Jesus' endurance provides the ultimate example for believers.
2. Recognize that perseverance is possible only when our focus stays on Christ.
3. See how Jesus' joy and obedience reveal the purpose behind suffering.
4. Identify practical ways to "run with endurance" by following His example.
5. Commit to finishing the race of faith with steadfastness and hope.

# Introduction

THE CHRISTIAN LIFE IS OFTEN LIKENED TO A RACE. It requires endurance, focus, and perseverance. In Hebrews 12, the author encourages believers who are growing tired from persecution and hardship. He reminds them that others have run the race before them, the heroes of faith in chapter 11, but then points them to the ultimate example: Jesus.

The command is simple but powerful, *"Keeping our eyes on Jesus."* When we lose focus, we stumble. But when we fix our eyes on Him, we find strength to keep going. Jesus not only started the race of faith; He completed it. He trusted His Father completely, obeyed perfectly, and endured faithfully all the way to the cross.

What sustained Him was "the joy set before Him," the joy of pleasing the Father and bringing salvation to His people. He endured shame, pain, and rejection because He saw the purpose behind it. His obedience was not easy, but it was perfect. Now, seated at the right hand of God, He reigns as both our example and our encouragement.

When life gets tough, it's easy to lose hope. But Hebrews 12 reminds us that Jesus has already gone ahead of us. He understands what it's like to feel tired, misunderstood, and tested. Still, He never gave up. His victory assures us that we can finish the race too, because the same power that carried Him carries us.

## *Historical Background*

The book of Hebrews was written to Jewish Christians who were struggling with discouragement and pressure to abandon their faith. Many had faced rejection, persecution, and loss for following Jesus. The writer encourages them not to turn back but to keep going, fixing their eyes on Christ.

In Hebrews 12:1–3, he uses the imagery of a race surrounded by a "great cloud of witnesses." These witnesses are the men and women of faith from chapter 11, people who trusted God despite great trials. But above them all stands Jesus, the ultimate example of endurance.

The phrase "pioneer and perfecter of faith" means that Jesus is both the source and the finish of our faith. He paved the way, showing us how to trust and obey, and He completed the race, making it possible for us to follow. His endurance on the cross wasn't just physical; it was spiritual. He faced separation, shame, and scorn, yet He never wavered.

The author emphasizes Jesus' joy as the reason behind His suffering. "For the joy that was set before Him, He endured the cross." That joy was not in the suffering itself but in what it would accomplish—our redemption and His victory over sin and death. His suffering wasn't pointless; it served the greatest purpose of all. By fixing our eyes on Jesus, we can find the strength to endure any trial. He not only provides an example to follow but also the grace to do so. The One who began our faith will also complete it.

## Keep Your Eyes on Jesus

The first instruction in Hebrews 12:2 is clear: *"Keeping our eyes on Jesus."* It's a call to focus. The Christian race is filled with distractions: fear, fatigue, failure, and the temptation to quit. But endurance begins with focus. When our eyes are on Jesus, we run with clarity and purpose. When we look at our circumstances, we lose strength.

The early Christians who first read Hebrews grew weary. They had endured suffering for their faith, and some were starting to doubt. The writer reminds them, and us, that the key to finishing the race is not found in looking inward but upward. Jesus is both the starting point and the finish line of our faith. He is the "pioneer," the One who blazed the trail ahead of us, and the "perfecter," the One who completed it perfectly.

To "keep our eyes on Jesus" means to focus our attention and love on Him. It's more than a glance; it's a steady stare. It involves consistently viewing everything through the lens of who He is and what He has done. When Peter walked on water, he remained steady as he looked at Jesus, but he began to sink when he looked at the waves (Matthew 14:29–30). The same is true for us. Where we focus determines our endurance.

Jesus' life demonstrates what it means to trust God fully. He lived with consistent obedience, even when it meant going to the cross. He didn't let the opinions of others, enemy opposition, or the weaknesses of friends pull Him away from His mission. His focus remained on doing the Father's will.

For us, this focus is both a command and a comfort. It means that when we grow tired, we have a place to turn. We are not asked to rely on our own strength but to draw from His. Looking to Jesus reminds us that He has already endured everything we face, and overcome it. Keeping our eyes on Christ doesn't mean ignoring pain; it means seeing purpose beyond it. It means trusting that the same power that carried Him through suffering now lives in us. The race is long, and the hills are steep, but our Savior has already finished it. He runs beside us, strengthening us to endure.

If you want to stay faithful in a world full of distractions, fix your eyes on the finish line that already stands: Jesus, the author and perfecter of your faith.

## Endure with Joy in the Midst of Suffering

Hebrews 12:2 says that Jesus, *"for the joy that lay before Him, endured the cross, despising the shame."* Those words reveal something astonishing about our Savior. He faced the worst suffering imaginable, the weight of sin, rejection, pain, and humiliation, yet He did so with joy. The joy wasn't in the agony of the cross itself, but in what the cross would accomplish. Jesus saw beyond the suffering to the salvation it would bring.

The cross symbolized both physical suffering and public shame. Crucifixion was meant to humiliate as much as to kill. Yet Jesus *"despised the shame."* That means He overlooked it. He refused to let temporary humiliation define His eternal victory. He endured because He knew what was beyond it: the redemption of the lost, the defeat of sin, and the glory of His Father.

This view changes how we handle our own trials. Suffering loses its power to harm us when we see it from the perspective of purpose. Jesus didn't avoid suffering; He defeated it through obedience. The same Spirit that strengthened Him now lives in us, allowing us to endure with hope.

The "joy that was set before Him" included both His return to the Father and the redemption of His people. It was the joy of obedience fulfilled, love completed, and victory secured. That joy was greater than the pain. His focus on the eternal gave Him endurance in the temporary.

We often seek joy after facing trials, but Jesus found joy through them. True joy doesn't rely on comfort; it depends on confidence in God's plan. When we suffer for righteousness, serve despite hardship, or endure pain, we follow Christ's example. The joy ahead: the hope of resurrection, reunion, and reward, gives us strength to keep going.

The Christian life will have its challenges. But because Jesus endured, we can also endure. Because He finished, we can finish. The joy of pleasing God and fulfilling His purpose is much greater than the shame or struggle we might face along the way.

To endure with joy means trusting that God's story is still unfolding. What seems painful now may be shaping something wonderful later. Jesus' joy was not in what He endured, but in what His suffering achieved. That same joy can empower us when faith feels difficult. When we fix our eyes on Jesus, we remember that endurance isn't just surviving, it's trusting. Like our Savior, we can face trials with steady hearts, knowing that the end of the race holds joy worth every step.

## Follow His Example to the Finish

Hebrews 12:3 urges us to *"consider Him who endured such hostility from sinners against Himself, so that you won't grow weary and give up."* Those words remind us that Jesus is not only our Savior, but He is our example. He shows us how to finish well when the race is long and the struggle is real.

The word *"consider"* means to think carefully, to weigh, to focus the mind. The writer encourages us to examine closely Jesus' endurance, His patience under pressure, His faithfulness under fire, and His obedience during suffering. He faced hatred, betrayal, mockery, and violence, yet He never lost heart. When He was insulted, He didn't retaliate. When He suffered, He entrusted Himself to the Father's will (1 Peter 2:23).

Following Jesus' example means running the same kind of race, with endurance, humility, and trust. We're not promised an easy path, but we are promised His presence. He has gone before us, and He runs beside us. Every time we feel like quitting, we are invited to "consider Him," to remember His strength, His patience, and His faithfulness.

Those who first read Hebrews were tempted to give up because of persecution. Their faith was costly. But the writer wanted them to know that Jesus endured far greater hostility and conquered it. If He could endure the cross, then they could endure their trials. And if they followed Him faithfully, they would share in His victory.

Jesus didn't just begin the race; He finished it. He endured the cross, rose from the grave, and "sat down at the right hand of the throne of God." Sitting down means the work is done. Redemption is complete. The race is finished. And now He intercedes for us, giving strength to all who run after Him.

To follow Jesus' example means more than admiring Him; it means imitating Him. It means responding to hardship with faith, meeting opposition with love, and trusting that every step brings us closer to the joy set before us. The same endurance that carried Him through the cross can carry us through every trial. Faithfulness to the finish is possible because Jesus has already finished for us. He paved the path, provided the power, and secured the victory. Our task is to keep running, to refuse to grow weary and give up.

When you feel worn down, remember the One who endured for you. When you are tempted to quit, remember the One who never did. The finish line is closer than it feels, and Jesus stands there, waiting with open arms, saying, "Well done."

## Lesson Summary and Reflection

The writer of Hebrews calls us to endurance, but not in our own strength. Our example and encouragement come from Jesus Himself. He ran the race of faith perfectly, endured suffering completely, and now reigns in victory eternally. When we grow weary, we look to Him. When we lose focus, we fix our eyes again on His faithfulness.

First, *keep your eyes on Jesus.* The Christian life is full of distractions, but focus gives endurance. Jesus is both the beginning and the end of our faith, the One who started it and the One who will complete it. Looking to Him keeps us steady when the path grows hard.

Second, *endure with joy amid suffering.* Jesus faced the cross not with despair but with joy; the joy of pleasing His Father and saving His people. He looked beyond the pain to the purpose. We, too, can endure hardship when we remember that our suffering is never wasted. God uses it to shape our hearts and advance His glory.

Third, *follow His example to the finish.* Jesus endured hostility, betrayal, and shame but never gave up. He finished His race and sat down at God's right hand. He is now both our example and our helper. His victory guarantees ours. The same strength that sustained Him is available to us through His Spirit.

The message of Hebrews 12 is clear: don't give up. The road of faith is difficult, but we are not alone. We run surrounded by witnesses, strengthened by grace, and guided by the perfect example of Jesus. The finish line is certain because He has already crossed it for us.

### Key Truths

- Endurance begins with focus—keep your eyes on Jesus.
- Joy in suffering comes from trusting God's purpose, not avoiding pain.
- Jesus endured hostility and shame to bring us victory and hope.
- Faithfulness to the finish requires daily dependence on His strength.
- Our Savior not only showed the way—He now helps us walk in it.

# Conclusion

Jesus is the power that enables us to persevere. He ran the race before us, carried the cross for us, and secured eternal life for us. When we fix our eyes on Him, our faith finds strength, and our steps find purpose.

The call of Hebrews 12 is to stay in the race. Don't look back. Don't give up. Keep your eyes on the One who finished His course in perfect obedience. Because He endured, you can endure. Because He overcame, you will overcome.

Faithful endurance isn't about running fast; it's about running focused. Keep your eyes on Jesus, and you will finish strong.

# Memory Verse and Weekly Challenge

**Hebrews 12:2 (CSB)** — *"Keeping our eyes on Jesus, the pioneer and perfecter of our faith. For the joy that lay before Him, He endured the cross, despising the shame, and sat down at the right hand of the throne of God."*

Endurance comes not from looking at our struggles but from fixing our gaze on Jesus—the One who ran the race perfectly, suffered willingly, and finished victoriously.

### Weekly Challenge

1.  **Refocus Your Eyes.**
    Each day this week, begin your prayer time by reading Hebrews 12:1–3. Ask God to help you keep your eyes on Jesus rather than your circumstances.

2.  **Find Joy in Obedience.**
    Choose one act of service or sacrifice to do quietly this week, focusing on pleasing God rather than being noticed.

3.  **Endure With Purpose.**
    When something frustrates or discourages you, pause and pray, *"Lord, help me see the purpose behind this."* Let endurance replace frustration.

4.  **Encourage a Runner.**
    Reach out to someone who's growing weary in their faith: perhaps through a note, prayer, or visit. Remind them that Jesus endured for them and still runs beside them.

5.  **Celebrate the Finish Line.**
    Spend time in worship reflecting on Christ's completed work. Thank Him that because He finished His race, you can finish yours.

# For Discussion

1. What does it mean for you personally to "keep your eyes on Jesus" in daily life?

_____

_____

_____

2. How does remembering the joy that sustained Jesus help you face your own challenges?

_____

_____

_____

3. When are you most tempted to give up or lose focus in your walk with God?

_____

_____

_____

4. How can you learn to see trials not as punishment but as preparation for endurance?

_____

_____

_____

5. What practical step can you take this week to run your race with more focus, faith, and perseverance?

_____

_____

_____

# Conclusion

The journey through these lessons has traced a clear theme: God shapes His people for service. From Noah's obedience to Jesus' perfect example, we've seen that faith is not built in comfort but in trust, obedience, and endurance. Every servant we studied was called, tested, and strengthened for a greater purpose. And through their stories, one truth has remained constant: *God equips those who are willing.*

Each lesson revealed a different facet of what it means to be equipped for God's work:

- **Noah** showed faith that obeys before understanding.
- **Abraham** taught us to trust God's promises even when the path is unclear.
- **Moses** reminded us that God uses humble, reluctant hearts to accomplish His will.
- **Joshua** proved that courage grows from confidence in God's promises.
- **David** showed that preparation often happens in quiet, unseen places.
- **Nehemiah** taught that a burden for what's broken can become a call to rebuild.
- **Daniel** modeled conviction that stands firm in a shifting world.
- **Mary** revealed the beauty of surrender and trust in God's plan.
- **Peter** displayed the power of grace to restore what failure breaks.
- **Paul** embodied boldness born from conviction and grace.
- And finally, **Jesus** stands as the perfect example of faith, obedience, and endurance.

Together, their lives tell a single story: God forms His servants through faith and uses them to bless others. Every example, flawed or flawless, points us back to His purpose: that we might be "complete, equipped for every good work" (2 Timothy 3:17).

What we've studied together over the last thirteen weeks is an invitation. God still calls His people to live by faith, to lead with courage, to serve with compassion, and to finish with endurance. The same Spirit that empowered these men and women works in us today.

As you close this study, ask yourself:

- What has God been preparing me for?
- Where is He calling me to serve?
- How will I use what I've learned to strengthen others?

God's work in you is not finished. Every act of obedience, every prayer of surrender, every moment of endurance is part of His ongoing plan to shape you into a servant who reflects His glory.

*Now may the God of peace, who brought up from the dead our Lord Jesus— the great Shepherd of the sheep—equip you with everything good to do His will, working in us what is pleasing in His sight, through Jesus Christ, to whom be glory forever and ever. Amen."*
**Hebrews 13:20–21 (CSB)**

www.ingramcontent.com/pod-product-compliance
Lightning Source LLC
LaVergne TN
LVHW010320070426
835513LV00025B/2432